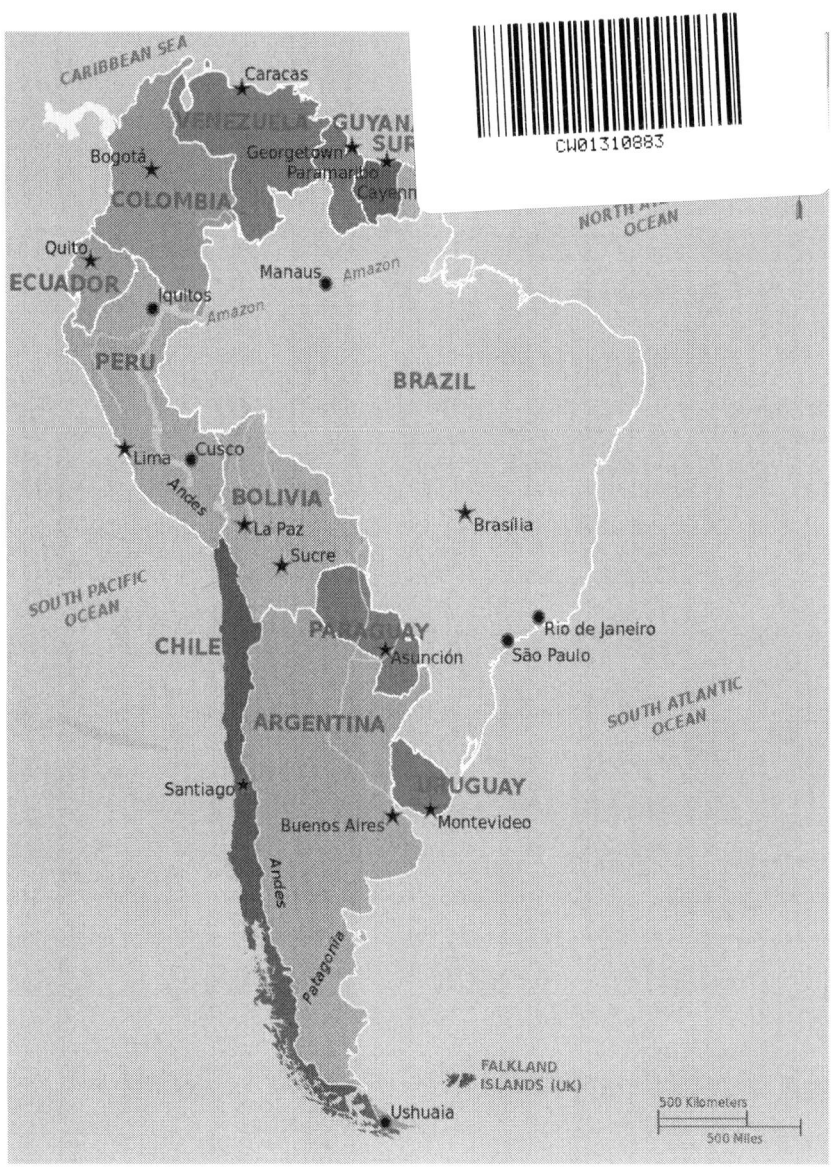

Contents

Prologue - Jumping on another Bus 4

1) Backpacking in South America - An Introduction 6
    1.1 Why South America? 6
    1.2 Snapshot Country Summaries 6

2) Things to do before your Trip 11
    2.1 Do some Planning and Background Research 11
    2.2 Get any necessary Vaccinations 12
    2.3 Get Travel Insurance 14
    2.4 Book a Flight to South America 16
    2.5 Get a Backpack and pack 19

3) Suggested Backpacking Route 23
    3.1 Cartagena to Uyuni (Colombia, Ecuador, Peru & Bolivia) 23
    3.2 San Pedro de Atacama to Punta del Este (Chile, Argentina & Uruguay) 37
    3.3 Porto Alegre to the Amazon (Brazil) 47
    3.4 The Best of the Rest 52

4) Visas & Border Crossings 56
    4.1 Entry Requirements 56
    4.2 Border Crossings 62
    4.3 Getting to/from Central America 65
    4.4 Yellow Fever Certificates & Return Tickets 67

5) Budgeting 70
    5.1 Money 70

5.2 Typical Backpacking Costs in South America	74
5.3 Ten Tips for Sticking to a Shoestring Budget	77
6) Fiesta!	**82**
6.1 Top 10 Festivals - Where & When	82
6.2 Best Party Destinations	85
7) Best Places to Experience Local Culture	**87**
7.1 Top 5 Places for Indigenous Culture & Ancient History	87
7.2 Top 5 Traditional Dance Destinations	88
7.3 Top 5 Football Cities	90
8) Best Destinations for Adventure & Nature	**93**
8.1 Five Activities for Active Travellers & Adrenaline Junkies	93
8.2 Five Natural Wonders	94
9) First Time Travellers in South America - FAQ's	**96**
9.1 Buses & Getting Around	96
9.2 Local Lingo	98
9.3 Staying Safe	99
9.4 Finding Accommodation & Making Friends	103
9.5 Weather & When to go	105
10) About	**107**
10.1 About Funky Guides	107
10.2 About this Guide	107

Prologue - Jumping on another Bus

Backpackers tend to land on South American soil for the first time with a mixture of excitement about unravelling Incan mysteries and exploring breathtaking scenery, as well as a touch of trepidation about what's in store as they begin their travels in a continent which is casually branded as dangerous by just about everyone.

Whether you arrive in Bogota or Buenos Aires, Lima or Sao Paulo, the initial impressions as you begin what will probably be a slow and unnecessarily lengthy journey through horrendous traffic and unpleasant neighbourhoods into the first city centre of your trip will probably be negative. The writing might be in Spanish but the suburban slums of South America are a long way from the elegant streets of Madrid and the glitzy bars of Barcelona.

With the odd exception, large urban areas in these parts can be fairly nightmarish places but few people come to this continent for the megacities that tend to dominate life in their respective countries. Indeed many travellers opt to skip them altogether and in pursuit of 'the real South America' they climb mountains, explore ancient ruins, trek days through jungles and above all spend an awfully long time on buses!

That's right, South America is an enormous and rather complicated place to get your head around so whatever you come for it's unlikely you'll find the answer overnight. Curiously it's those long, occasionally spectacular but frequently monotonous bus journeys that provide time for reflection and often offer up the biggest clues to unravelling this continent's hidden secrets, both past and present.

As you travel further away from the cities and climb slowly into the altitude of the Andes where so much South American history has been shaped, people change, faces change and the hand of time seems to unwind with every passing mile. There'll be hours where you see virtually nothing and then all of a sudden pass a humble Indian dressed as they would have been centuries ago working on the same small coca plantation that their fathers and grandfathers would also have worked on.

A few miles down the road and you'll pass yet another white cross signifying the spots where lives have been lost as cars, trucks and somewhat ominously buses have gone tumbling off the cliffside. After an hour or so you might even reach a small town or village but it will probably look just like the dozens of other small Andean settlements you have passed through.

This isn't postcard South America nor is it likely to make it onto travel shows or youtube 'best of' clips. There's no flamenco, samba, beaches or Brazilian bottoms but this is the South America as millions on this continent know it and this will be the backdrop for weeks of travelling as you weave in and out of the seemingly endless Andes which stretch a magnificent 7,000 kilometres from Venezuela's Caribbean coastline to the freezing Southern shores of Argentina.

So you better get ready to leave all preconceptions at passport control because in a split second, often when you least expect it, South America can surprise, inspire and occasionally shock you but it will certainly make you think and often it is the smallest, seemingly most insignificant moments when memories are made.

1) Backpacking in South America - An Introduction

1.1 Why South America?

Travelling in South America is more challenging than doing likewise in Europe or even many parts of Asia which have ready-made travel scenes that go out of their way to make you feel like you've not left home. That's not really the case in South America and to many that is a huge part of its appeal. It's unapologetically raw with eye-opening sights, both positive and negative at almost every twist and turn.

The continent has a little bit of everything and is so big that anyone can find a small corner of it that is right up their street. Without stepping foot on an airplane it is possible to go from the beautiful Caribbean coastlines of Colombia and Venezuela, cross the world's largest jungle, travel thousands of kilometres down the world's longest mountain range before hitting the remarkable lakes and glaciers of Patagonia and eventually reaching the southernmost city on our planet just a metaphorical stone's throw from icy Antarctica.

Throw into the mix fascinating ancient cultures and some of the best preserved archaeological sites on Earth and you'll also be treated to a wonderful history lesson. Add to that passionate people, pulsating parties and rapidly changing cities with everything from desperate poverty to extreme luxury and you have a toxic mix that ensures your time in South America will be lively if nothing else.

South America is not for everyone, nor does it strive to be but travellers who learn a bit of the lingo and get stuck in often find themselves falling in love with this continent and some end up staying for months or even years longer than they had originally planned.

1.2 Snapshot Country Summaries

Colombia

Colourful Colombia is fast becoming a hit with backpackers thanks to its welcoming people, stunning coastlines and surprisingly hip cities. In the early years of the 21st Century, all but the most foolhardy of travellers went to Colombia but it has largely lost its dangerous reputation and in reality is probably safer than neighbouring Ecuador and Peru that have always received hordes of travellers. The narcos and FARC rebels have been suppressed and the second most populous country in South America is reinventing itself. A must visit for those looking for a lively fusion of Latin passion.

Ecuador

Considerably smaller than most of the other countries in South America it may be, but Ecuador packs a lot into a small space. It is more like three separate countries squeezed into one, each with wildly different climates. The coastal areas are home to some chilled out beach towns such as Montañita which boasts great surf and one of the best backpacker party scenes on the continent. Moving inland you reach the snow-capped Andean peaks and the historic cities of Quito and Cuenca. Continuing west it's not long before you are heading down again, this time into the depths of the Amazon.

Peru

Much of Peru is a dusty dry arid landscape which can begin to become more than a little bit monotonous after your umpteenth hour on an uncomfortable bus. However your patience will eventually be rewarded with some of the most incredible relics of life gone by that anyone could wish to see. The Inca Trail to Machu Picchu is far from the only such one but it is the undisputed travel highlight of the country and reaching the summit of the ancient Inca civilisation is perhaps the most memorable moment of any trip to South America.

Bolivia

The continent's poorest country is full of shocks and eye-opening moments, some of them pleasant, some of them less-so. From a budget traveller's perspective landlocked Bolivia is paradise, with meals and beds available for less than US$2 and a culture that is about as far-removed from the developed West as it gets in this part of the world. Travel highlights include a trip to the world's largest Salt Flats which is a weirdly wonderful experience, while at the other end of the country the incredible Lake Titicaca is full of myths and legends at 4,000 metres above sea level.

Chile

Possibly the most oddly shaped country on the planet, there are only really two directions in Chile, north and south. Head west and before too long you find yourself encountering the blustery winds and chilly waters of the Pacific. Head east and you'll very quickly encounter the dizzy heights of the Andes which separate it from Argentina. This lanky strip of land is home to two of the continent's hippest cities in the form of Santiago and nearby Valparaiso, some stunning national parks, frozen glaciers, fiery volcanoes and dusty deserts. If you can deal with the ridiculous distances of getting from one to the other, a good time is guaranteed. Thankfully the recent emergence of budget flights has made backpacking around Chile a more manageable experience.

Argentina

Around a third of Argentines live in the metropolitan area of Buenos Aires which completely dominates the political and economic landscape in this country but of more interest from a travel perspective, it is also arguably the most exciting city on the continent. There is plenty more to Argentina than BA though, however you will have to cover some ground if you want to find it. Thousands of kilometres south from the bustling capital you reach the stunning Lake District and the giant glaciers of Patagonia. Head west towards the Andes and you get to the glorious vineyards that produce some of the world's best wine while just about anywhere you can tuck into a great steak and Argentina is an absolute must for culinary lovers.

Uruguay

Frequently described as South America's most liveable country, little Uruguay consistently punches above its weight. Despite a population of just over 3 million people, this football mad country has twice won the World Cup and while it may lack the ancient history of some of the others, it has some of the continent's best beaches, nightlife and a surprising amount of things to see and do.

Brazil

Almost half of South America's land mass is Brazil and over half of its people are Brazilian. It has a very different vibe to the rest of the continent, not just because Portuguese is the dominant language as opposed to Spanish. The world famous carnival celebrations in Salvador and Rio de Janeiro show off the country at its uninhibited best but come any time of the year and the beaches and bubbly inhabitants will have you captivated. Away from the coast and despite an enormous amount of deforestation, the Amazon still looms large and a trip deep into the rainforest is another thing that should be high on your 'to do' list.

Paraguay

Landlocked Paraguay isn't particularly popular with travellers and the closest most get is a visit to the stunning Iguaçu Falls which separates the country from Brazil and Argentina. It has some interesting religious sites and has managed to maintain much of its indigenous heritage but perhaps the biggest appeal is that it is just so far removed from the main South American traveller trails that wherever you are in Paraguay, you can still claim to be 'off the beaten track'.

Venezuela

Usually in the news for all the wrong reasons, not many travellers venture into Venezuela these days which is a shame because it has plenty to offer but it's also not particularly surprising given the continent's Northernmost country is not known for being the safest place to be. Outside the main cities which can be fairly unpleasant (same can be said of most big cities in South America), there is some wonderful nature including table-top mountains, huge waterfalls, spooky caves and some 600 Caribbean islands, many with outstanding beaches.

French Guiana, Guyana and Suriname

For starters many people don't even realise that these three countries are in fact part of the South American mainland. They are more Caribbean than South American in their culture and customs and as former colonies of France, Britain and Holland respectively, the languages spoken reflect that (you'll need to brush up on your Dutch before you hit Suriname). French Guiana is still officially a French overseas territory but the other two are now independent.

They aren't easily fitted into a South American backpacking trip due to their isolated location, sandwiched between Venezuela and the also rarely visited extreme north of Brazil. Besides a few small towns on the coast, all three are very rural and sparsely populated but nature lovers, trekkers and fans of peace and tranquillity might just find their paradise here.

2) Things to do before your Trip

2.1 Do some Planning and Background Research

This guide should hopefully help you a fair deal with that but you'd be wise to do your own research into the places you are heading or thinking about heading to. The backpacking routes in the next section might be a useful starting point if you're looking for inspiration.

General things to bear in mind here are that you will spend a lot of time travelling between different places and many first-time travellers in South America make the mistake of being far too ambitious when it comes to trying to fit too much into a short amount of time. Taking long night buses every other night is fine for a week or so but after several months it can start to become more of an ordeal than a fun travelling experience.

You would probably need about a year to travel to and have a relatively full experience in all the countries in South America. Although the larger nations such as Brazil, Argentina and Chile now have more affordable domestic flights, travelling across international borders by air is still usually very expensive. Therefore unless you have that sort of time on your hands or money to burn, you will really have to pick and choose which countries you visit.

Here's a useful plan to follow in this phase:

1. Decide how much money you have or are willing to spend on the trip.

2. Decide how much time you have. Perhaps you know this already due to work, study or family commitments. If you have no fixed date that you need to get back for then how much time you have will probably just be a question of how quickly your money is going to run out. Section 5.2 of this guide on backpacking costs in the different countries should give you an idea of how to go about answering what is actually quite a difficult but important question.

3. Once you have a budget and a timespan in mind, read up on the countries and decide upon what your priorities are. If your budget isn't huge then consider sticking to the Andean countries like Bolivia, Peru, Ecuador and Colombia that form the basis of many backpacking routes in this region and are quite a lot cheaper than Brazil and Chile for example.

4. Come up with a very rough plan for your route. This is by no means something you need to stick to exactly but you'll need to have this in mind when you book your flights to South America. Given its size, it's useful to have at least a start and end point in mind and make sure you have enough time and money to get from one to the other and still be able to make your flight home.

2.2 Get any necessary Vaccinations

As always the best advice is to speak to a medical professional at your local doctor's surgery or health centre and describe your plans in as much detail as possible. They are likely to then tell you which vaccinations are recommended for your trip although ultimately it is up to you which ones you get. Be aware that opinion often differs even between medical practitioners about which vaccinations are absolutely essential in South America so it might be worth trying to speak to a few different people if possible before making a judgement.

In general travellers in South America typically require fewer vaccinations than those in less developed parts of Asia or Africa for example. However if you haven't done much travelling lately the list can still potentially be quite long and depending on the cost of these things in your country, quite expensive. This is something you should ideally do a couple of months prior to your trip as you may need to take a course of jabs and it can also take time for the vaccinations to kick into effect.

Here are some of the most common diseases that travellers need to be aware of and depending on your circumstances consider seeking preventative treatment against before visiting South America.

Yellow Fever

This is important, not least because it can be a deadly disease (caused by mosquito bites) but also because many countries officially require you to be vaccinated against it before they will allow you to enter their country (more on this in section 4.4). Although the certification is rarely asked for, just about every traveller heading to South America is recommended to have the yellow fever jab because the risk areas are quite extensive.

Chile and Uruguay are the only countries considered completely free of yellow fever. All of Paraguay, Suriname, Guyana and French Guiana carry a risk. As do almost all inland and some coastal regions of Brazil. East of the Andes in Bolivia, Peru and Ecuador there is a risk while over 90% of Colombia and Venezuela also fall into the danger zone. Unless you've been to Africa or South America before, you won't have been vaccinated against Yellow Fever so this is one you'll probably have to get.

Risk areas have actually been extended in recent years following large outbreaks in Brazil in 2017 which have seen even the major states of São Paulo and Rio de Janeiro experiencing cases.

There is a map of the latest risk area here -
www.cdc.gov/yellowfever/maps/south_america.html

Diphtheria, Tetanus and Polio

It's advisable to make sure you are still protected against these diseases and although you may well have had these vaccinations in the past, if it has been over ten years since the last one, a booster dose is generally recommended. On the positive side, protection against this trio is usually combined into just one jab.

Typhoid, Hepatitis A, Hepatitis B, Tuberculosis

You might be surprised to find you are actually already protected against some or perhaps all of these diseases from vaccinations you had as a child or for previous trips abroad. If not then it just comes down to exactly where you're planning on going, what type of trip you're looking to have and for how long.

Ultimately the medical professional you speak to will be making something of a judgement call based on the perceived risks as to whether or not they recommend you to get vaccinated. Generally they will be over cautious and tell you to get vaccinated against these diseases even if the actual risks are very low so It's up to you whether you listen or not but clearly it's better to be safe than sorry!

Rabies

Doctors often recommend travellers to get the rabies jab which can be quite expensive but many South American backpackers opt to skip this and with some justification. The rabies jab doesn't make you immune from the disease, it only increases the amount of time you have to seek treatment in the event of a bite. Unless you're trekking deep into the jungle where you may be 24 hours away from emergency healthcare then it's not really essential that you get it. Regardless of whether you do or don't get the jab, it is important to seek medical help as soon as possible if you get bitten by what you suspect might be a rabid animal.

Malaria

The Amazon basin is the main risk area so if you are planning on heading into the jungle you will probably need to get some form of malaria tablets. If you're not going into the Amazon then malaria isn't really much of a problem.

This Amazon basin risk area includes much of Northern Brazil and some rural parts of Guyana, Suriname, French Guiana, Venezuela, Colombia, Ecuador, Bolivia and Peru. However most of the main cities and travel destinations are malaria free, as is just about everywhere in the Andes where the altitude is too high for Malaria to flourish.

Suggested reading for health info in South America:
www.fitfortravel.nhs.uk/destinations#south-america-antarctica

Note that even if you have Malaria tablets and get the Yellow Fever jab, it is still highly advisable to take precautions against mosquito bites in the high-risk areas. Use insect repellent and where practical keep your arms and legs covered. At night, try to stay in places with mosquito nets over the beds and keep doors and windows shut.

2.3 Get Travel Insurance

Getting insurance that covers you against the sort of things that can go wrong in South America is also very important. Travel insurance for a backpacking trip is very different from typical holiday insurance. This is because the trips tend to be much longer, usually including visits to various countries and perhaps even including a range of activities that can occasionally lead to injuries or illness. These kind of things are often not included in regular travel insurance packages so it is important to carefully check what is covered before you book anything.

The continent also has, as you're probably aware, a somewhat dangerous reputation and this is not entirely undeserved. You are very unlikely to come to physical harm yourself unless you seriously go looking for it but theft is undeniably a problem in many places.

Most of this is petty and can be avoided by being vigilant and taking good care of your belongings and not flashing expensive phones and cameras. Electronics are very expensive in South America so they are attractive to thieves and if yours get stolen, you won't be able to replace them cheaply and you are unlikely to be assisted much by the police who usually have bigger problems to deal with than a gringo losing their iPhone. This sort of thing is annoying at the time but you can usually claim the money back later via decent travel insurance. Of course the best solution is just not to bring expensive items in the first place but many travellers do.

On a more serious note, there are very occasional cases of buses getting held up by armed gangs and everyone on board being relieved of their belongings. You are incredibly unlikely to come to any harm yourself in rare instances like this but obviously losing your backpack would be a fairly major disaster! Having proper travel insurance is a lifesaver if something like this was to happen although by avoiding night buses in known problem areas like Western Colombia and following local advice, you can generally avoid such issues.

There are only a few major companies that really specialise in providing cover for backpackers. World Nomads, True Traveller and World First all have insurance geared towards people on gap years or trips of multiple months. World Nomads offers perhaps the most extensive cover and might be the safest bet while World First is generally a cheaper alternative but it's worth checking the terms closely. Depending on where you're from, there may be smaller national insurance companies that offer better deals so do your research!

www.worldnomads.com | www.truetraveller.com | www.worldfirst.com

2.4 Book a Flight to South America

You need to think carefully about your plans when you book your flight to South America which will probably be by some distance the most expensive purchase of your trip.

Depending on the length of your stay and how much ground you aim to cover, it may be better booking a single or return ticket. Returns are usually cheaper but chances are it will leave you needing to take a connecting flight within South America to get back to your original destination to fly back home. Given that international flights within South America can often be as much as the cheapest flights to Europe or North America it may be better just to book two separate flights which allows you much more flexibility in any case.

Officially you need a return ticket to enter many countries in the region however in reality this is incredibly rarely asked for. If in doubt speak to the airline you intend to fly with and make sure they will allow you to board the plane with just a one-way ticket. More details on this topic in section 4.4.

To begin your search, start looking on a flight comparison site like skyscanner.com several months before your trip. Looking too far in advance or leaving it too late is likely to lead to inflated fares. Try to be as flexible as possible when it comes to your dates e.g. choose a month rather than an exact date when you search.

It's also an idea (especially if you're a student or under 26) to look on Sta Travel (www.statravel.com) as they often have special youth deals on flights that don't appear in searches on flight comparison sites. They also have options that are tailored to backpackers such as multi-city trips where you fly in and out of different cities, possibly with flights in between and multi-flex passes which enable you to make changes to your bookings when you're out on the road.

One other option to consider for anyone from North America, Europe or

Asia is to book a single or even return flight to Miami, which is generally viewed as the best place to fly to South America from, with the biggest range of options. Consider spending a few days in Miami and then connecting to a flight, with some decent budget links to South America available from nearby Fort Lauderdale.

These are some of the main routes into South America:

From Europe

TAP - Portugal's international airline has the largest number of flights of any European airline into Brazil and connects Lisbon to a host of cities right across its former colony.

IBERIA - Plenty of flights from Madrid to almost all the major South American cities.

KLM - Directly connects Amsterdam with Suriname as well as a few other key South American cities like Buenos Aires, Rio and Lima.

AIR FRANCE - Connects Paris to French Guiana as well as Rio de Janeiro and Lima.

CONDOR - Can be the cheapest option with lots of flights from Frankfurt (connections to dozens of other European cities available) to Buenos Aires, Bogota, Cartagena, Lima and a large number of cities, primarily coastal in Brazil. Check they will allow you to travel with a one-way ticket though as this is a holiday company, primarily targeting families on short visits.

This list is by no means exhaustive and there are direct flights to South America from London, Zurich, Rome, Milan, Istanbul and other European cities. Some South American airlines also now operate flights to Europe too.

From Oceania

AEROLINEAS ARGENTINAS - Direct flights between Buenos Aires and Auckland with connections to Australia.

LATAM - Also cross the Pacific but direct from Auckland and Sydney to Santiago. If you're heading this way, you could consider stopping in

Tahiti and/or Easter Island on the way.

QANTAS - Fly from Sydney and Auckland to Santiago.

Going the other way around, there are longer flights to South America from Perth via stopovers. For example you can fly from Perth to Rio via Dubai with Emirates with the whole trip taking about a day.

From North America

SPIRIT AIRLINES - This US budget airline has reasonably priced flights into Colombian cities like Cartagena and Bogota from Florida's Fort Lauderdale airport and one service to Lima and the Ecuadorian city of Guayaquil.

JETBLUE - Another budget airline to have entered the market for highly sought after US to South America routes and they fly to cities in Colombia, Ecuador and Peru including Bogota and Quito from Fort Lauderdale or Orlando with excellent connections across the United States.

There are also direct flights via the more expensive national airlines in Mexico, Canada and Panama from Mexico City, Toronto and Panama City respectively into some of the main cities in South America. You can also now fly direct from a host of US cities into South America's major hubs including Atlanta, Dallas, Houston, New York, Charlotte, Orlando, and Washington.

LAN, TAM and Avianca are among the South American airlines to offer flights into North America from their regional bases.

In short there are now lots of options for travellers between the two continents but it's always worth checking out what the prices would be if you were to book two separate flights, changing in Miami (or Fort Lauderdale) which is still the main connection between the two.

From Asia

EMIRATES - Some of the longest non-stop flights in the world go from Dubai to São Paulo and Rio de Janeiro with the latter continuing on to Buenos Aires.

QATAR AIRWAYS - Non-stop 16 hour service from Doha to São Paulo continuing on to Buenos Aires.

Note that it is really a rather long way from Asia to South America so allow for at least a day of travelling in most cases, especially if you have connections at either end. The direct flights mentioned above are unlikely to be your cheapest options with connections in Europe or USA likely to work out better. Anyone in the Far East will need to connect to a flight, most likely in a US airport such as Los Angeles.

From Africa

SOUTH AFRICAN AIRWAYS - Fly direct from Jo'burg to São Paulo.

ETHIOPIAN AIRLINES - Fly direct to São Paulo from Addis Ababa which is handy for anyone looking to combine some travelling in East Africa and South America.

TAAG ANGOLA AIRLINES - Flights from Luanda to São Paulo.

ROYAL AIR MAROC - Fly direct from Casablanca to São Paulo and Rio with affordable connections onto many European cities available.

Overall though options are limited for getting from Africa to South America and flights are infrequent.

IMPORTANT - When booking it is usually cheaper to book via an online travel agent than directly on the airline's website. This is a little ridiculous but it is usually true. Use a flight comparison site like skyscanner to find the best deal as there are dozens of websites that sell flight tickets and the price can sometimes vary considerably.

2.5 Get a Backpack and pack

Getting a good backpack is a prerequisite for any trip of length but it is especially important in South America where you will be spending plenty of time getting from A to B. It should be sturdy and waterproof, but crucially you should also be comfortable carrying it.

Shop around, visit a few places (camping stores are a good start) and try lots of backpacks on until you find something you are happy with. If it feels too heavy with nothing in it, then it almost certainly will be when you finish packing! The key is finding the right balance between strength and comfort. Something with a few different compartments is handy for separating dirty and clean clothes, as well as storing your valuables and documents somewhere that isn't going to be easily reachable for pesky pickpockets and thieves.

Once you're sorted, you can start to think about packing which isn't an easy process if you've not done much travelling before. You really don't need to pack as much as you might think given there are pretty cheap launderettes everywhere in South America as most families don't have a washing machine. That said there are plenty of things you need to consider.

A long trip in South America, no matter when you go is likely to see you experience a wide range of weather conditions, often even on the same day. Many of the most popular destinations are at altitude where the sun is strong and days are usually warm, but after dusk the temperature can drop dramatically meaning you will need a sufficient supply of warm clothes too.

If you're planning on doing a fair bit of trekking either in the jungle or the mountains, you'll need a sturdy pair of boots but most of the other gear can be rented or bought on location to avoid weighing down your backpack to ridiculous levels. A lightweight waterproof jacket is certainly a good idea too as it's highly unlikely that you're going to beat the rain for your entire trip. Ultimately it comes down to where you're planning on going and what kind of trip you're looking to have but regardless a range of different clothing is a good idea, just not too much.

Electronic items aren't essential but in reality virtually everybody takes a mobile and it does at least allow you to keep in touch with people at home more easily while offering many advantages in terms of using apps to get around and see things whilst relieving boredom on longer journeys. It's also an idea to unlock it before you leave home so you can use a local sim in any countries you will be spending several weeks in.

˥e backpackers take laptops or tablets (most hostels will have wifi of ᴺuality) but unless you have a specific reason for doing so, it's not really necessary and there are also internet cafes everywhere. If you take expensive electronic items then it's worth forking out to stay in slightly better places that are more secure and certainly don't stay in dorms that don't have lockers.

Regardless of what you end up packing, make sure you are able to carry the damn backpack before you head off to the airport as you are basically going to be living out of it and carrying it everywhere for the duration of your trip. If it feels heavy to begin with, it will be much harder when you're in hot conditions or at energy-sapping altitude trying to figure out where the hell your hostel is.

A few key things that are a good idea to pack regardless of which part of the continent you're heading to:

Money - Obviously you need money but money you can't access is pretty useless so take some emergency cash (US Dollars are most useful) and preferably at least two other sources of funds in case you have problems with using cards at ATMs. Store them in different places if possible. If you go out at night try just to take a sufficient amount of cash for the night and leave everything else in a safe place (a locker if you're in a dorm).

Documents - Passport, flight tickets, photocopy of your passport, record of any vaccinations you've had (remember your yellow fever certificate), a few passport sized photos, travel insurance confirmation.

Clothes - 7-10 days' worth of clothes is adequate (with a mix of cooler and warmer wear) but nothing ridiculously heavy or so flashy that you'd be devastated if it got lost or damaged. Don't expect to return home with everything you came with!

Towel - Don't assume that your hostel will provide you with towels. Most don't.

Toiletries - Just bare essentials like toothpaste, toothbrush, and shower gel. Buy more when you run out.

First aid - Plasters, sun protection, diarrhoea pills, headache tablets, contraception.

Small lock - Important. Perhaps take two, one for your bag and one for your locker if you're planning on staying in dorms.

Earplugs - Again very handy for sleeping in dorms or on buses.

Power adaptor & charger(s) - You can get worldwide adaptors quite cheap these days and they are your best option as the type of sockets vary between countries in South America. Also remember to pack chargers for any electronic item you end up bringing as finding a replacement can be tricky as there's no guarantee that the same model of your phone/camera will be sold in the countries you visit.

3) Suggested Backpacking Route

There are three routes in this chapter although if you have enough time, they join together to make one huge itinerary covering the best the continent has to offer. If you have less than 6 months to complete your trip then choose bits that appeal or just use it as a little bit of inspiration for forming your own itinerary.

It's generally better not to have a completely rigid plan in mind before you set off on your trip though. Things can change quickly once you hit the road so use it as a guideline to a fairly typical path that budget travellers in South America might take rather than the definitive solution.

The more 'comfortable backpacker budget' quoted in each section allows you a bit more room for extra activities, slightly better hostels or a greater amount of partying. The shoestring budget is much tighter and is based on you staying in the cheapest places, travelling always the cheapest way and almost always eating/drinking in cheaper local joints or cooking for yourself.

Note the accommodation suggested in all sections of this backpacking route is where possible based on places that are cheap, sociable and have consistently received good reviews from travellers. Most are really good value but cheaper places can usually be found if you are on a real shoestring budget and don't mind a back-to-basics experience.

3.1 Cartagena to Salar de Uyuni (Colombia, Ecuador, Peru & Bolivia)

time : 3 months

shoestring budget : $2500 | €2200 | £1950

more comfortable backpacker budget : $3500 | €3100 | £2750

COLOMBIA

1. Cartagena (3 days - 1 week*)

Cartagena is easily accessible from Florida which has excellent links to the rest of the world so it's a good starting part and an incredible introduction to South America. It's a historic city with a beautifully preserved old town but also a lively multi-cultural vibe. It's close to plenty of Caribbean beaches too and is an all-round fun place to hang around for a few days or more.

suggested accommodation: Hostel Mamallena, 10-47 Calle Media Luna, Getsemani

*One good option for anyone with limited español is to take an intensive week of Spanish classes. There are plenty of language schools in Cartagena and many private teachers who will do reasonably based one-on-one lessons to explain at least some basic phrases and vocab you may need on your trip.

2. Tayrona National Park (3+ days)

Stunning national park with perfect Caribbean beaches, loads of nature and plenty of hiking opportunities. It's not the easiest place to get to but it is worth it! First head to the somewhat tacky holiday resort town of Santa Marta and then take a connecting bus into the park. Be careful when swimming as there are some seriously dangerous currents in these waters.

suggested accommodation: Not really a place with advanced online booking options so just show up and you'll find something. Tents and hammocks can easily be rented cheaply while nicer bungalow-type accommodation is also available.

3. Lost City Teyuna AKA Ciudad Perdida (4-5 days Trek)

This is one of the best treks in South America to a mysterious ancient city in the Colombian jungle. It's a bit like Machu Picchu but not on the top of a giant mountain and without the hordes of tourists! Trips can be arranged in Santa Marta and it is a 46 km round trek through the jungle and typically takes 3-5 days. There are loads of chances to stop and get close to the wildlife and nature on the way to the lost city.

Note that it is almost impossible to visit the Lost City independently and organised treks cost around $300 in total so shoestring travellers may want to give this one a miss unless it massively appeals. If you want to do both this trek and another one or two multi-day organised trips in Peru or Bolivia for example, then certainly the 'more comfortable backpacker budget' should be your basis for budgeting.

suggested accommodation: Organised by trek company.

4. San Gil (3 days)

The highlight is not the town but the surrounding nature. This is an adventure sports hot spot with cheap and excellent rafting, paragliding, hydrospeeding and waterfall abseiling amongst the options but there are also plenty of routes for more tranquil bike rides and hikes.

suggested accommodation: Hostal Le Papillon San Gil, Calle 7, Number 8-28, Santander

5. Cocuy National Park (2-3 days)

Another beautiful national park with many snow-capped peaks and plenty of wildlife including bears, deer, pumas, condors and rabbits.

suggested accommodation: Hostal El Caminante, Cra. 4, #7-30, El Cocuy

6. Villa de Leyva (1 day)

Historic and very pretty colonial town with an enormous central plaza, one of the largest in the world. You won't need much more than a day to see it all but it's a nice stop on the way to Bogota.

suggested accommodation: Magma Z, Carrera 8, #15A-21

7. Bogota (2-4 days)

Welcome to the madness that is a South American capital city. Bogota is an enormous place and is changing rapidly and mostly for the better. It has the best museums in the country and some of the best in South America so it's well worth spending a few days here and discovering one of the continent's hippest and most happening cities. Most of the hostels are in or near the old La Candelaria district which has become a bit of a hipster hangout.

suggested accommodation: El Pit Hostel, Carrera 5 #26C-82

8. Salento (2 days)

Salento is a really pretty town but admittedly quite touristy by Colombian standards although most of the visitors are from other parts of Colombia. Some of the highlights here include visits to local coffee plantations, the stunning views from the town's miradors and hikes into the misty Valle de Cocora. For the lovers of all things weird, go check out some pig racing!

suggested accommodation: Luciérnaga Salento Food Drinks Music Hostel, Carrera 3 #9-19

9. Cali (2 days)

Colombia's pumping salsa city is home to some excellent nightlife, especially at the weekend. It's a bit rough around the edges and there is little really to see but if you get stuck in you can have a fantastic time and make plenty of new Colombian friends.

suggested accommodation: Mango Tree Cali, Cra 5 #6-32

10. Popayan (1-2 days)

Perhaps the most attractive of Colombia's old towns. It has a ridiculous number of churches and pretty white buildings in a small area and is the only place west of Cali that has much going for it before you reach Ecuador.

suggested accommodation: HostelTrail, Carrera 11, Number 4-16

BORDER CROSSING

Ipiales (Colombia) - Tulcán (Ecuador)

Getting from Popayan to the Ecuador border is sometimes dangerous at night with armed bandits in Western Colombia prone to holding up buses and stealing things. Therefore set off early in the morning and consider stopping overnight in Pasto or Ipiales although it is possible to reach Otavalo on the same day. Speak to the manager at HostelTrail for up-to-date info on this.

The border crossing itself is fairly quick and painless and one of the most spectacular in South America. All you have to do is wander over the international bridge to get from the Colombian emigration post to the Ecuadorian immigration one. Take a short taxi or minibus from Ipiales bus terminal to the border crossing and do likewise once you've cleared immigration in Ecuador and head to the nearby town of Tulcan from where there are regular direct buses to Otavalo and Quito.

ECUADOR

11. Otavalo (2-3 days)

Famous for its enormous Saturday market and friendly indigenous people. It's a wonderful place to experience traditional local culture and has some beautiful hills, rivers and waterfalls around the town which are easy to explore. On a very different note, the weird and quite brutal sport of cock-fighting is a popular pass-time here for locals, the odd backpacker and well, anyone who likes seeing chickens going at each other with razor blades.

If that doesn't sound like your idea of fun, then check out the quite unique dress sense of the Otavalenos. Both the men and women usually sport long ponytails and they seem to have held onto their traditions much better than most of the other indigenous groups in this continent.

suggested accommodation: El Andariego Otavalo, Bolivar 12-10 between Quiroga & Salinas

12. Quito (3 days)

Ecuador's famous capital city. The old town has plenty of character and streets to explore while there are literally hundreds of museums with the excellent Museo del Banco Central perhaps the highlight. You can take the teleferico to get a breathtaking look over the whole city. At night, the more modern La Mariscal district really comes alive with lots of restaurants, bars and discos.

suggested accommodation: Blue House, Joaquin Pinto E8-24 y Diego de Almagro

13. Cotopaxi (OR Tena & Puyo) (3-4 days)

There are two very different routes you could take between Quito and Baños. The first takes in the stunning National park near Latacunga with the freezing peaks of the enormous 5900m Volcan Cotopaxi at the centre of it.

Alternatively you could take the jungle route which is a bit longer via the small towns of Puyo and Tena which are on the fringes of the Amazon but you can head deeper into the jungle via trips from the towns.

suggested accommodation for Cotopaxi: Hostal Cafe Tiana, Luis. F. Vivero 1-31 y Sanchez de Orellana, Latacunga

suggested accommodation for Tena & Puyo: These jungle towns are both very small and pretty friendly so just walk around and look for a cheap room.

14. Baños (2-3 days)

Touristy town but a very pleasant safe place with its famous baths. Baños is surrounded by green mountains and there are loads of different ways to experience the nature. There are plenty of rivers and waterfalls in the area so it's a nice place to hang around for a few days and explore. It is also a popular stop with travellers so a small backpacker nightlife scene has developed.

suggested accommodation: Great Hostels Backpackers, Ricardo Zurita Carrillo y Ambato (900m from bus & train station)

15. Riobamba (1-2 days)

Mountain town surrounded by snow-capped peaks. It is the starting point of the steep and spectacular train ride down to Sibambe which is one of the must-dos of travel in Ecuador. Once you reach the end in Sibambe, it's probably best just to head straight to Cuenca as there isn't much there.

Some travellers also head to the coast afterwards for the chilled out atmosphere at the beach party town of Montanita but it's a fairly long trip by Ecuadorian standards at least.

suggested accommodation: Hotel Puertas del Sol, Avenue Luis Cordovez 22-30 y Espejo - This is a pretty unremarkable budget hotel but it's one of the cheapest options in town with no real backpacker-type places.

16. Cuenca (2-3 days)

A lively riverside city full of colonial era buildings and nice places to eat and drink. It is home to the Northernmost Incan ruins and several cathedrals and is the sort of place that just oozes history. It is also very bicycle-friendly with many hostels and travel agencies offering cheap rentals.

suggested accommodation: Mallki Hostel, Calle Aurelio Aguilar 1-31 y Av. Solano. Cuenca has a wide choice of options for budget travellers so you shouldn't have any trouble finding a decent place here.

BORDER CROSSING

Huaquillas (Ecuador) - Aguas Verdes (Peru)

There are direct buses from Cuenca to Northern Peru along the Pan American Highway including a stop in Mancora which are said to be in the region of $15 and take around 7 hours at night but longer in the day with a company called Azuay. The buses stop at the border for you to complete entry/exit formalities which are now conducted in the same building.

The direct buses are a relatively new thing and have relieved much of the hassle out of this crossing. If for some reason you'd prefer to do it all yourself, take a bus to Huaquillas and then cross the international bridge to the town of Aguas Verdes, Peru from where there are plenty of buses heading south. Mancora is not a massive destination for Peruvians but most buses heading to bigger towns like Piura and Trujillo will drop you off there if you ask.

PERU

17. Mancora (2-3 days)

Popular beach resort full of drunk gap year students, surfers and lively party hostels. Either it's your thing or it's not! Beware of thieves on the beach.

suggested accommodation: Misfit Hostel, Avenida Playa el Amor, Ld 25

18. Chiclayo (2-3 days)

Here you can visit the excellent Museo Tumbas Reales de Sipan (in a nearby town) and explore the Pomac forest on horseback. There are several other ancient sites and tombs nearby with remains of ancient civilisations well preserved in part thanks to the dryness of the desert.

suggested accommodation: Hostal Satelite, Av. Pacífico 494

19. Trujillo (1-2 days)

Truth be told, Northern Peru has little in comparison to the south but Trujillo is a decent stopover for a day or so with the ruins at Chan Chan and the Moche Pyramids among the most popular things to visit. They're not as impressive as Machu Picchu by any stretch of the imagination but are more extensive and cover a large area so if you're a fan of ruins you will enjoy it. Travellers often opt to stay outside the city centre at the beach of Huanchaco.

Consider then flying down from one of the Northern cities to Cuenca or Arequipa and skip what is probably close to a couple of days of bus journeys when it's all added up. If you're on a tight budget and can't find a cheap flight then you might just have to suck it up and there are a few cool stops along the way.

suggested accommodation: Ugarte Hostels, Alfonso Ugarte 445

20. Huaraz (2-3 days)

Into Peru's central Sierra now and the dizzying heights of Huaraz (altitude sickness tablets at the ready). Popular things to do here include trekking and rock climbing in the surrounding mountains. There is though some surprisingly good nightly entertainment and live music and there are growing numbers of travellers although not all backpackers in Peru come this way.

suggested accommodation: Vacahouse B&B, Ramón Mejía 710, Parque FAP-Huaraz

21. Lima (2 days)

The capital of Peru is impressively perched on huge cliffs above the crushing waves of the Pacific Ocean. It's okay for a few days but for a capital city there's not really that much to see and do beyond the odd cool neighbourhood to explore. Also like most big cities in South America there are several no-go areas where crime is a big problem and travellers are easy targets.

Most travellers stay in either the districts of Miraflores or Barranco. You should be able to find great Peruvian cuisine in either and Peruvian food and drink is widely viewed as among the best in South America with tasty dishes such as ceviche and lomo saltado, washed down with a pisco sour.

suggested accommodation: Hostelima, Coronel Inclan 399, Miraflores

22. Huacachina (1-2 days)

The tiny town of Huacachina is not the place to learn about Peruvian history and culture as it only really exists for the benefit of travellers and tourists but it has a few pretty cool things going for it. The main attractions are the enormous sand dunes that surround the somewhat manufactured lakeside town.

To go deep into the dunes you have to take one of the bumpy dune buggy rides but if you can master the frustratingly fine art of sandboarding (it's basically like snowboarding but on sand) then you're sure to have plenty of fun. Failing that just use your board like a sled and hurtle down the dunes while trying not to kill yourself.

suggested accommodation: The New Desert Nights Hostel, Balneario de Huacachina 139

23. Nazca (1 day)

Famous for its mysterious lines as featured in Indiana Jones. Unfortunately flyovers are out of the budget of most backpackers and it's not that impressive from the ground. However without stopping here, it's a very long bus ride to Cusco and it's still a lengthy night bus from Nazca. Consider flying from Lima to Cusco if you have the funds to do so.

suggested accommodation: Nanasqa Hostel, Calle Los Geranios L13,

Amaprovi

24. Cusco (3 days)

Cusco is a wonderfully historic city and is a UNESCO world heritage site with beautiful plazas and ancient buildings. It is very popular with travellers so there are lots of tourist facilities and it is a good place to arrange trips to Machu Picchu. Certainly one of the highlights of travel in Peru.

suggested accommodation: Inka Wild Hostel, Calle Matará 261

25. Machu Picchu & The Inca Trail (4-5 days)

Perhaps South America's most iconic destination. There are lots of ways to reach the ancient Incan city and you can do it as a 7 day trek via more sites if you like but the 4 day option is the most popular. Be prepared to pay quite a bit for this trip as it is obviously one of the most popular travel destinations in the world. You'll need to head back to Cusco afterwards to continue your journey.

There is a full list of licensed tour operators here - www.incatrailperu.com/inca_trail_tour_operators.html

If you opt to hike up to Machu Picchu with a tour company, you won't need accommodation as your tour operator will sort all that out (forget trying to stick to the 'shoestring budget' if you take this approach). If you do it all yourself then the nearest town with accommodation is Aguas Calientes and it has a number of hostels, although expect to pay a bit more than you might in the rest of Peru. This is still by far the cheapest way to visit Machu Picchu.

suggested accommodation: Don Andre, Calle Wiñaywayna 110, Las Orquideas, Aguas Calientes

26. Colca Canyon (2-3 days)

Home to one of the world's deepest canyons, this is another of Peru's most popular travel destinations and a great spot for hiking. You can do it as a trip from Arequipa but there are plenty of budget rooms to be found in nearby Chivay and Cabanaconde as well as at the bottom of the canyon itself.

suggested accommodation: Villa Pastor, Plaza de Armas S/N, 054 Cabanaconde

27. Arequipa (2-3 days)

The most important city in Southern Peru and in many ways much nicer than the capital Lima. There's lots to do here and the giant El Misti volcano which hovers over the city makes for a challenging climb. In town there are some fascinating sites relating to the town's mysterious past including the famous Juanita Mummy which you can see in the Museo Santuarios Andinos.

suggested accommodation: Arequipay Backpackers Downtown, Pasaje O'Higgins No. 224, Vallecito

28. Puno (1/2 days)

There's not a great deal in Puno but it's on the banks of Lake Titicaca and it's nice to stay for a day or two and check out the incredible Lake from the Peruvian side before making the short trip across the border into Bolivia.

suggested accommodation: Kantaya Hostel, Santiago Giraldo #220

BORDER CROSSING

Yunguyo (Peru) - Copacabana (Bolivia)

It's very easy to get from Puno to Copacabana with public buses although many travellers opt for the affordable direct tourist buses at 7:30am and 2:00pm (en.incalake.com/bus+puno+copacabana+la_paz) taking about 3-4 hours including the time spent at the border. The bus will first drop you at the Peruvian exit post and once everyone's stamped, transport you to the Bolivian one where the same procedure happens and then everyone boards for the 10 minutes or so it takes to reach Copacabana which is only 5 km from the border.

There isn't really a Bolivian town or settlement on the other side of the border before Copacabana but there are a few people trying to make a quick buck at the crossing by exchanging Sol for Bolivianos. There have also been reports of Bolivian border officers attempting to fine travellers for basically any excuse they can think of. Don't stand for any of that and if you find yourself in that position just hold your ground and be aware that Bolivia is a very poor country and there is a fair amount of corruption.

BOLIVIA

29. Copacabana & Isla del Sol (3-4 days)

The first town in Bolivia on the banks of Lake Titicaca. You can stay in town but be sure to spend some time on Isla del Sol which is said to be the legendary birthplace of the Incas and is accessible by a short boat ride from Copacabana. It's a beautiful island in the middle of the highest lake in the world at 3,800 km above sea level! Many travellers rate this as one of their highlights of South America.

A word of warning though as Bolivia is nowhere near as developed as any of the other countries on the route. Until relatively recently Copacabana had no ATM machine which isn't ideal when you're in a new country and need some local currency. Although there now is one, don't count on its reliability so bring US Dollars or a healthy amount of Peruvian Sol and get them exchanged in town.

suggested accommodation: Hostal Salome, Avenida La Paz 45

Accommodation in Bolivia is seriously cheap but often very basic. Most of the budget places have little to no web presence and can't be booked online. In Copacabana head to Avenida 6 de Agosto and search for a room.

30. La Paz (3-4 days)

One of the smallest, poorest and yet safest capitals on the continent. Busy street markets and the best museums in the country are some of the main attractions. There is also an incredible hike you can do nearby called El Choro Trek which starts in the mountains at La Cumbre (4700m) and ends in the jungle at Chairo (1500m). It is about 60 km though so would take several days but there are plenty of buses that do the route so the option to cheat a bit exists.

While in town pay a visit to the excellent Coca Museum which documents the history of coca production in the country and US-led efforts to thwart it. It'll make you think if nothing else and the same could be said for the notorious San Pedro Prison which weirdly has a long history as a backpacker destination although some recent efforts have been made to prevent visits. Read Marching Powder by Rusty Young for a fascinating and harrowing insight into life inside what is surely the world's most unusual prison. Speak to other travellers or your hostel staff for info on how to visit it as the situation changes regularly.

suggested accommodation: Loki La Paz, Av. Las Americas #120

31. Cochabamba (2-3 days)

Cochabamba is at a slightly lower altitude so days are a bit warmer although it still gets cold at night. It has become a bit of an adventure destination with great hikes and other activities in the hills around the town and there are some hot springs close by which make for a nice target.

suggested accommodation: Running Chaski Hostel, Calle España #449 casi Calle México

32. Sucre (1-2 days)

This relaxed town known as 'la ciudad blanca' is probably the most attractive in Bolivia. There are some lovely villages around it too such as Tarabuco (famous for its Sunday market) and Candelaria.

suggested accommodation: Villa Oropeza Hostel, Loa 737

33. Potosi (2 days)

Potosi is the highest city in the world at a huge 4 km above sea level and was once one of the richest thanks to vast natural resources in the Cerro Rico which to a large extent funded the vast Spanish empire. Now though it is desperately poor with few remnants of its heyday. One of the most memorable yet shocking things you can do in South America is head down the dangerous working mines in Potosi to experience the truly awful conditions that workers deal with on a daily basis. Tours are easily arranged in town or through your hostel.

suggested accommodation: Hostel Casa Blanca, Calle Tarija 35, between

34. Uyuni (for Salar de Uyuni Tour) (4 days)

The world's largest salt flat! It's best to head to the town of Uyuni and then arrange a 4x4 tour from there. Typically they take 3/4 days but shorter ones are possible and it is an awe-inspiring sight as you head towards the centre and literally all you can see is a vast whiteness. This is a photographers paradise and many backpackers celebrate by stripping down for a cheeky snap. You don't have to indulge in this slightly peculiar tradition but if you're going to take all your clothes off outdoors, this is probably as good a place as any!

suggested accommodation: This is one of the smallest towns on the route and gets a lot of visitors so there is plenty of accommodation. Get off the bus and walk around and ask to look inside places before finding one that seems reasonable and fairly priced. Some bargaining is acceptable and you'll probably only need to stay in town for a night before heading out into the Salar de Uyuni itself on the tour.

Speak with backpackers in Bolivia and ask around in town before settling on a tour as they vary greatly in price and quality. You can expect to pay between 600 and 1000 Bolivianos ($85-145) for a 3 day tour with some variation in prices depending on the season. It should be possible to book one that starts in Uyuni and drops you off in Chile.

There is good info here on what to expect from a 3 day Salt Flats tour - twomonkeystravelgroup.com/backpackers-guide-uyuni-bolivia-san-pedro-atacama-chile/

CONNECTING TO PART 2

Going from Uyuni to San Pedro de Atacama is a route many travellers take but very few locals do so there aren't any public buses that do the trip directly. There are a few buses a week from Uyuni to Calama, close to San Pedro de Atacama and they take about 12 hours including the border crossing at Abaroa (Bolivia)/Ollague (Chile).

Some of the tours of the Salt Flats enable you to be dropped off at the Chilean border on the final day which is useful if you are following this route. From there you can more easily take a bus to the city of Calama and then it's relatively easy to get to San Pedro de Atacama via buses that take 2 hours or so.

3.2 San Pedro de Atacama to Punta del Este (Chile, Argentina & Uruguay)

This route sees you continue to travel southwards down the Andean regions of Chile and Argentina to the glorious lakes and glaciers of Patagonia before ending up in a city that prides itself on being known as 'the end of the world'. From there you turn around and head north for the first time in many months and to Buenos Aires, perhaps the most exciting city in South America. Then it's a short hop into Uruguay to complete this leg of the journey.

Camping and hitch-hiking is about the only way to do this section of the route on a similar budget to the first. Both are very possible and are worth considering. If not, you are likely to be spending a fair bit more in 2 months here than you did during 3 months on the first route.

Chile and Argentina are both very large countries and they are both over 4000 km long from their northern borders to icy southern tips. Therefore it takes a long time to cover it all over-land. Buses are usually the cheapest options (besides hitch-hiking) but there are budget airlines that run between all the main cities. Sky Airline (www.skyairline.cl) and Latam (www.latam.com) are the main options in Chile and prices have reduced dramatically in recent years making it a much easier country to navigate on a shoestring budget. For the Argentine sections, Andes Lineas (www.andesonline.com) or LADE (www.lade.com.ar) may be your best bets and it's worth checking the cost of flying before booking any long distance buses, although factor in any additional baggage fees, which can be high on budget airlines.

Our suggested shoestring budget is essentially based on taking buses on every leg with the exception of Ushuaia to Buenos Aires which is likely to set you back between $100-150 with LATAM normally offering the cheapest fares. On the bright side, the buses are considerably more comfortable than the ones in Bolivia and Peru and the scenery is often spectacular.

The more comfortable backpacker budget below allows you much more freedom to take a few flights to save time and should let you do many more organised activities and trips.

time : 2 months

shoestring budget : $3000 | €2650 | £2350

more comfortable backpacker budget : $4500 | €4000 | £3500

CHILE

1. San Pedro de Atacama (2-4 days)

To get here you will probably need to change buses in Calama and from there it should be about 2-3 hours by bus to San Pedro de Atacama. There is a stunning, almost otherworldly landscape around the laid back but somewhat expensive (for South America) town. You can see the more immediate surroundings on horseback or by bicycle and it is one of Chile's most popular travel destinations.

Highlights including taking a 'star tour', the Geysers del Tatio as well as the Lunar and Death Valleys although there is a limit to what you can do independently on a budget as many of the main sites of interest are a long way out of town with no public transport connections.

suggested accommodation: Hostal Laskar, Las Parinas 478

2. La Serena (2-3 days)

Plenty to do in and out of this coastal town. One of the highlights is the Elqui Valley, home to an incredibly clear night sky, perfect for stargazing. It is also where you can find some of the longest stretches of beaches in all of Chile and often they are almost deserted.

suggested accommodation: Open Hostel La Serena, matta 315

3. Vina del Mar (2+ days)

Vina del Mar is a stylish city home to one of the most popular beaches in the country although it can be a bit chilly if you're there in the winter months (June to August). It also plays host to one of South America's biggest music festivals each February and is literally only 10 minutes down the coast from Valparaiso, the next stop on this route but both places warrant their own visits.

suggested accommodation: Jaguar Hostel + Living, Pasaje 2 Poniente No. 333, Casa 12

4. Valparaiso (2-3 days)

120 km or so west of Santiago lies the Pacific Ocean and the vibrant city of Valparaiso, a really colourful harbour town and one of the most popular backpacking destinations in Chile. It has a big bohemian feel to it and as you roam around the hilly streets you'll never be far from something quirky. Valpo has some of the best street art in South America and Museo La Sebastiana, the former home of Chilean poet Pablo Neruda is a must visit. It's also surrounded by excellent vineyards with tours available and the locally produced but world famous Chilean wine is well worth a taste.

suggested accommodation: Planeta Lindo, Almirante Montt 677, Cerro Alegre

5. Santiago de Chile (2-3 days)

The capital of Chile is one of the most beautifully located capitals in the world with the Andes mountains providing the stunning backdrop. They provide plenty of great trekking opportunities and you can even go skiing not too far from Santiago. The city itself is enormous and one of the biggest on this route so it's the best place to buy anything you might need for your trip to the wilderness of Southern Chile and Argentina. It has also developed into a thriving cultural centre and there is a reasonable amount to see and do without leaving the confines of the city but 2-3 days should be sufficient.

suggested accommodation: Che Lagarto, San Antonio 60

Getting from Santiago de Chile to the Lake District is the first in a series of long journeys you'll need to do to reach the Southern tip of this incredible continent. It is around 750 km between Santiago and Villarrica so it's a bit of a mission. Most travellers opt to take a night bus (buses leave daily) and this will save you a night on accommodation. It is also possible to fly from Santiago to Temuco which is about 30 minutes by road from Villarrica, the first destination in the Chilean lake district.

6. Villarrica (3-4 days)

Villarrica is surrounded by lakes, volcanoes, caves and hot springs and is a very popular hiking destination. In the summer it can be nice to stay in Pucon, a small beach town on the banks of Lake Villarrica. You can also explore the area by horse or go on rafting trips. The highly active Volcan Villarrica (which explosively erupted as recently as 3rd March 2015) is a stunning sight but trips up it are very much restricted because as you might imagine it can be fairly dangerous!

suggested accommodation: Hostal Casa Ajedrez, Isabel La Católica 350

From Villarrica southwards all the way to Ushuaia camping becomes a good option (certainly in summer) as it is very rural so it might be worth investing in a lightweight tent and you'll save plenty on accommodation which can be quite pricey in these parts, especially during the peak summer months.

7. Cochamó Valley (2-3 days)

Hiking, rock-climbing, ridiculous valleys and cliffs as well as some rather wonderful natural waterslides are all the rage here. You can get to Cochamo by taking a bus from Villarrica to either Puerto Varas or Puerto Montt and then transferring onto a bus into the isolated Cochamo Valley which has limited lodging options but camping is possible for those who like it wild.

suggested accommodation: Las Bandurrias Eco Hostal, Sector el Bosque s/n

8. Chiloe Island (3 days)

It doesn't really matter whether you head to Cochamo or Chiloe first as to access either you need to pass through Puerto Varas or the larger Puerto Montt. Chiloe is the largest island in Chile with more incredible scenery and treks as well as some lovely little villages and plenty of intriguing ancient myths.

suggested accommodation: Hostal Altos de Gamboa, Manuel Jesús Quinchen s/n, Castro

Chiloe Island is a big place and the town of Castro has the widest choice of budget accommodation so is probably the best base.

9. Puerto Varas (2 days)

A compact and unremarkable town but a decent base for more Lake District adventures. Options include the Vicente Pérez Rosales National Park, home of the Petrohué falls and Lake Todos los Santos. The giant Osorno and Calbuco volcanoes are also nearby. Mount Osorno has a pretty cool chairlift which is open all year round and is used by skiers in the winter and pretty much anyone who likes a nice view in the summer. Kayaking and rafting are also possible close to Puerto Varas and it is your best base for getting to Argentina.

suggested accommodation: Casa Apel Hostel, Eleuterio Ramirez 415

BORDER CROSSING

Paso Cardenal Antonio Samoré (Chile - Argentina)

As the crow flies there is little more than 100 km between Puerto Varas in Chile and San Carlos Bariloche in Argentina. However with some rather large mountains and plenty of lakes in the way, crossing the Andes is not such a simple task. There are daily direct departures with the Andesmar (www.andesmar.com) bus company at 8:55am costing about $20 and taking roughly 6-7 hours including a stop at the border post known as Paso Cardenal Antonio Samoré which is one of the better organised of the Andean crossings between the two countries.

Alternatively there are some companies that offer ridiculously named but more direct bus-boat-bus-boat-bus-boat-bus crossings (or something like that). The deal is that you cross over the Andes via three stunning lakes and take in some truly breathtaking scenery while typically stopping overnight at a village in the Andes somewhere between the two. However prices tend to be well over budget as far as most backpackers are concerned with some costing as much as $300.

ARGENTINA

10. San Carlos de Bariloche & Nahuel Huapi National Park (4-5 days)

The long trip here will soon be worth it when you start exploring the beautiful Argentine lakes and mountains. It is famous for skiing, water sports, trekking and climbing. The town itself is also one of the liveliest in Patagonia, with a swanky Alpine-resort vibe and some banging bars and clubs that party on past dawn. It is certainly an essential and usually very popular stop on any Patagonia backpacking route.

suggested accommodation: Marcopolo inn Hostel, Salta 422

11. Esquel (for Los Alerces National Park) (2-3 days)

Esquel is 300 km or so south of Bariloche and is used as the gateway for Los Alerces National Park. It has loads of great hiking trails and extends right up to the border with Chile. The park takes its name from the alerce trees which are literally everywhere. The town itself is small and growing but has nowhere near as much going for it as Bariloche.

suggested accommodation: Casa del Pueblo, San Martin 661

Getting from the Lake District to the Extreme South is yet another long trip. There is a 24 hour bus that runs between San Carlos de Bariloche and El Chalten. One of the stops is Esquel so you can hop off and hop on the bus at Esquel where you can spend a few days. Prices vary but expect to pay around US$5 for every hour of travel. The ride is long but passes through some stunning, deserted scenery. Before long you realise you really have entered the weird wilderness of the far south of this continent.

12. El Chalten (2+ days)

This is a major hiking destination in the Southern Andes with ambitious trekkers taking on the challenge of Mount Fitz Roy and Cerro Torres, two of the biggest peaks in Patagonia. It's busy in the summer but pretty quiet the rest of the year apart from a steady stream of travellers backpacking through Argentina and Chile.

suggested accommodation: La Comarca Hostel. Perito Moreno 70

13. El Calafate (for Los Glaciares National Park) (2-3 days)

Just 2-3 hours by bus from El Chalten, this is also a major base for travellers in Argentine Patagonia looking to explore the fabulous Glaciers National Park. Entrance to the park isn't cheap and is only valid for a day but plenty of different boat trips and excursions can be arranged in El Calafate to witness the enormous glaciers close up.

suggested accommodation: Hostel de las Manos, Egidio Feruglio 59

BORDER CROSSING

Paso Río Don Guillermo (Argentina - Chile)

There are buses that take around 5 hours to get from El Calafate to Puerto Natales in Chile with Bus Sur (www.bussur.com) and Cootra (www.cootra.com.ar) costing around $25.

Some tour companies advertise direct buses to Torres del Paine but it is generally cheaper to head to Puerto Natales and make your way to the park from there. Hitchhiking from El Calafate to Puerto Natales is also very possible.

The border crossing is typical of those between Argentina and Chile, up in the Andes and with no town on either side of it, instead just an unremarkable couple of isolated buildings where immigration and emigration procedures take place.

CHILE

14. Puerto Natales (1-2 days)

There is nothing particularly amazing about Puerto Natales but it has good basic infrastructure for backpackers in Patagonia with plenty of hostels with dorm accommodation. It is an excellent base for making your way to Torres del Paine and Bernardo O'Higgins National Parks.

suggested accommodation: Hostel San Agustin, Arauco No. 629

15. Torres del Paine National Park (3 days)

Daily buses run to the Park from Puerto Natales and take around two hours. You are now really approaching the chilly Southern tip of the continent and Torres del Paine National Park is home to plenty of stunning mountains, glaciers, lakes, and rivers.

suggested accommodation: The little hostel-style accommodation there is in the park is extortionate with dorm beds sometimes going for over US$100 per night during the summer! There are plenty of campsites (some are free) and this is the best option if you want to stay overnight in the park although camping in non-designated areas is strictly not allowed. Ask around in Puerto Natales for recommendations of campsites or just head out to the park and follow signposts.

You will need to head back to Puerto Natales for the bus to Punta Arenas.

16. Punta Arenas (1-2 days)

Punta Arenas is the most southerly city on mainland South America. The weather can make exploring the town pretty difficult but there is a surprising amount of history and sites of interest. You can also get to the Seno Otway penguin colony where each spring hundreds of Magellanic Penguins come to breed. Meanwhile there is often a good view of some incredible whales from Carlos III Island.

suggested accommodation: Backpackers Paradise, Calle Ignacio Carrera Pinto, N.1022

BORDER CROSSING

San Sebastian (Chile - Argentina)

Punta Arenas and Ushuaia are linked by frequent bus services that take around 10-12 hours including a short ferry ride from mainland South America onto the island of Tierra del Fuego. The border crossing is just before the small Argentine maritime settlement of San Sebastian on Route 257.

There are also flights but these are much more expensive and miss out on some of the dramatic scenery. To get the most of that, travel by day with Bus-Sur's 8:30 a.m. departures a decent option, costing 35,000 CLP (roughly $50) and arriving in Ushuaia around 12 hours later.

ARGENTINA

17. Ushuaia (Tierra del Fuego) (3-4 days)

Ushuaia is commonly referred to as the southernmost city in the world and a thriving tourism industry has built up in recent years focused around the cruises to Antarctica. The town is now complete with nice restaurants and given its military history there are some cool museums to visit such as Museo Marítimo set in an old prison. Nearby Tierra del Fuego National Park is another incredible place to explore.

Making it all the way down to Ushuaia is becoming an almost rites of passage for backpackers in Argentina and indeed South America. It is possible to visit Antarctica from Ushuaia and it is the closest and easiest place in the world to access the 7th continent from. It's not cheap though and you'll need at the very least US$3000 and probably quite a bit more so it's not a realistic option for most budget travellers. Boats run between November and March and there is more info on this in Section 3.4.

suggested accommodation: Hostel Aonikenk, 25 de Mayo 576

While it is possible to head back north towards Buenos Aires by land, the route is far less spectacular than the Andean route you have just traversed and there are few obvious stops. Even by air it's about 3 hours 30 minutes to the Argentine capital from Ushuaia so you can imagine how long this trip might take by bus. It will set you back $100-150 for a flight but it's probably the only realistic option even for shoestring travellers unless you have developed a real passion for South American buses over the previous few months.

18. Buenos Aires (4+ days)

BA is arguably the most exciting city in South America with passionate locals and vibrant street life as well as great shopping and lively bars and clubs that only get busy well into the early hours of the morning and party past dawn on a nightly basis.

Then there are local obsessions like football and tango, both of which the city is world famous for. City lovers will finally rejoice that they have found somewhere pumping with life 24-7 after all that peace and nature. You can easily spend plenty of days exploring the different districts in the Argentine capital which dominates life in this country. Once you've had your fill of Buenos Aires, It's only a very short trip across the Rio de la Plata to Colonia in Uruguay.

suggested accommodation: Millhouse Hostel Hipo, Hipolito Yirigoyen 959

BORDER CROSSING (FERRY)

Buenos Aires (Argentina) - Colonia (Uruguay)

These two countries have always maintained close ties and given Uruguay is right on the doorstep of the Argentine capital and its 13 million residents, there is a lot of movement between the two countries. Several companies offer boat services, the quickest of which are catamarans that take just an hour to get from BA to Colonia while the slower but cheaper ferries take around 3 hours. Many tourists in Buenos Aires do this as a day trip given how close they are so be sure to just buy a single ticket (solo ida).

URUGUAY

19. Colonia (2 days)

A pretty cobblestone town very popular with travellers and day-trippers from Buenos Aires and one that has been named a UNESCO World Heritage site. It has a charming old town but can get a little overrun by tourists at weekends and peak times.

suggested accommodation: Celestino Hostel B&B, 18 de julio 380

20. Montevideo (2-3 days)

Small and very pleasant by the standards of capitals in Latin America. Montevideo has become very popular with artists and architecture lovers and it is often described as the most liveable city in South America.

suggested accommodation: Company Hostel, Emilio Frugoni 1126

21. Punta del Este (2+ days)

Home to some of the most popular beaches in South America and some very lively nightlife. For a quieter experience, head out to nearby Cabo Polonio, a tiny coastal village with sea lions, penguins and whales. How long you stay really depends on when you go (it's only beach weather from late November to mid April) and indeed how much of a beach lover you are. Either way you should be aware that it is also more expensive than the rest of Uruguay. Outside of the summer it's a pretty quiet place but things can get wild from December to February.

suggested accommodation: Tas D Viaje Hostel, Calle 24 entre 28 y 29

CONNECTING TO PART 3

Punta del Este is a popular destination with Brazilians so there are many connections to it from Brazil, especially in the summer months. However a distance of 750 km between the beach town and Porto Alegre makes it a fair old journey. There is an airport in Punta del Este but you will probably need to change flights in Buenos Aires to reach Porto Alegre so there's not much advantage in flying.

Most travellers opt to take one of the night buses which take around 10 hours. TTL (www.ttl.com.br) offers a night service leaving Punta del Este at 11:00 p.m. and arriving the next morning at 8:30am in Porto Alegre costing a pretty steep $75 or thereabouts. EGA (www.ega.com.uy) have a similarly priced service leaving at 9:30 p.m. and they also have a more expensive cama (bed) option. Those prices should give you a feel for how much more expensive bus travel in Brazil is compared to the other countries, although the costs are a bit higher in this case because it's an international service.

3.3 Porto Alegre to the Amazon (Brazil)

Brazil accounts for about half of this continent and you could easily spend 6 months travelling in the country and still not see anything like all of it. Our route obviously skips a lot out but gives you a little taste of the best beaches and cities as well as a fair slice of history and culture and ends up with an amazing boat trip along the Amazon River into the heart of the rainforest.

In Brazil it's also certainly worth checking the flights as sometimes you can fly for the same price or less than the lengthy buses. It is one of the few places in the continent where budget (or at least relatively cheap) airlines are a thing and if you want to visit several different parts of the country, flying becomes a necessity unless you happen to have several months spare and can afford the cost of backpacking around Brazil.

Cruz Azul (www.voeazul.com.br/en), GOL (www.voegol.com.br/en) and

Avianca (www.avianca.com) have some of the best fares for domestic routes in Brazil. Use a comparison site like skyscanner to figure out the cheapest option. Booking at least a couple of weeks in advance is advisable for the best deals.

By following the 'more comfortable backpacking budget' you will be able to take more flights and do more exciting trips and excursions, particularly in the Amazon. In the cities it will give you more freedom to get out and experience the famous Brazilian nightlife.

time : 1 month

shoestring budget : $1500 | €1300 | £1150

more comfortable backpacker budget : $2250 | €2000 | £1750

BRAZIL

1. Porto Alegre (2 days)

A nice city with a very strong European heritage and one of the richest in South America. Porto Alegre is a gentle introduction to Brazil and has a thriving music and cultural scene.

suggested accommodation: Porto Alegre Eco Hostel, R. Luiz Afonso, 276

2. Florianopolis (3 days)

A very popular coastal destination in Brazil with some of the country's finest beaches. A nice place to relax for a few days or more with a huge range of options when it comes to finding a spot to chill out for the day.

suggested accommodation: Floripa Surf Hostel, Srv. Ieda Maria Luz da Costa, 190, Campeche Beach

3. Ilha do Mel (2-3 days)

This island is a wonderful escape from the hectic big cities in Brazil with pleasant beaches and no cars or roads. It is usually really quiet during the week but gets much busier and livelier at the weekend and during holidays when residents of nearby towns and cities often flock to Ilha do Mel.

suggested accommodation: Hostel Encantadas Ecologic, Praia das Encantadas, 150 meters from the dock

4. Curitiba (2 days)

This cosmopolitan city in the south of Brazil has a rich history and is home to a mixed population that descends from various parts of Europe. It has a lively arts and music scene and an 'old city' district which is over 300 years old. It is also one of the safest and cleanest cities in Brazil.

suggested accommodation: Curitiba Backpackers Hostel, Rua Nilo Peçanha, 243

5. Foz do Iguaçu (2 days)

Possibly the most spectacular waterfalls in the world and a place where three countries meet. You can even pop over into Paraguay if you're looking to tick another country off your list!

There is an airport here also which is handy because the falls are a bit out of the way. If you're not too fussed or are short on time you could skip them and head straight to Sao Paulo or Rio from Curitiba but you would be missing out on one of the world's greatest natural wonders. Flying in from Curitiba and then onwards to Rio is preferable to spending 24+ hours on buses and not saving a great deal of cash. You can get flights from around 250 Reales (roughly $80) from Foz do Iguaçu to Rio although it's advisable to book a few weeks in advance as prices do go up significantly nearer the date of travel.

suggested accommodation: Hostel Manga Rosa, Avenue Florianópolis, 1085, Jardim Santa Rosa

6. Rio de Janeiro & Around (7 - 10 days)

The most famous and most recognisable city in South America. As well as the world class beaches, samba and Rio nightlife there are lots of great trips to do within a few hours of the city. Options include exclusive coastal resorts, party towns and mountain retreats with Paraty, Ilha Grande, Petropolis and Buzios among the most popular options. It's a good idea to take a few days to get to know Rio and then use the city as your base for exploring any surrounding areas that take your fancy.

suggested accommodation: Walk on the Beach Hostel, Rua Dias da Rocha 85, Copacabana

Rio is one of the most well connected cities in South America in terms of flights to Europe and other parts of the world and it is the natural end/start point for many travellers in South America. However if you have the funds and the time it's well worth spending another couple of weeks in Brazil and heading north and eventually moving into the depths of the Amazon.

It is again sensible to think about taking flights for the next two legs of the journey with large distances to cover. Rio to Salvador starts at about 300 Reales (roughly $80) with GOL (www.voegol.com.br).

7. Salvador (3 days)

Visiting Salvador means taking an extra flight instead of making the long leap north to Belem and the start of the Amazon. However it's well worth it to experience one of the most significant cities in Brazilian history. The state of Bahia is renowned for being friendly and easy-going and culturally there are strong African influences dating back to the Slave trade which is well documented in museums in Salvador. This city certainly moves to a different beat to those in the south and it is very evident with many bars serving up live music with a distinctly African beat. The carnival in Salvador is also fantastic and actually bigger than the one in Rio, claiming to be the biggest of its kind in the world.

suggested accommodation: Nega Maluca Guesthouse, Rua dos Marchantes 15, Santo Antonio/Pelourinho

8. Belem (2 days)

This is where you can start the long boat trip along the Amazon river. The town itself is worth staying for a couple of days perhaps and has some wonderful Portuguese colonial buildings but there's not an enormous amount to do other than gear yourself up for the jungle trip. When it comes to the Amazon, rivers are basically roads and boats of varying shapes and sizes are how both locals and travellers get around.

suggested accommodation: Belem Hostel, Rua Ó de Almeida, 624. Entre

Assis de Vasconcelos

9. Santarem & Alter do Chão (2-4 days)

Roughly halfway between Belem and Manaus this is a perfect place to break up what is a 4-5 day boat ride between the two cities. It is also close to what is often claimed to be Brazil's best beach despite it being nowhere near the sea (Alter do Chão is where the river beach is located). Although the boat rides are incredible experiences, they are not always the most comfortable so taking a few days break might be a wise move!

suggested accommodation: Hostel Pousada do Tapajós, Rua Lauro Sodré 100, Alter do Chão

10. Manaus & the Amazon (4+ days)

The biggest city in Amazonia, Manaus is a bizarrely large place, home to over 2 million people yet it is very isolated, located right in the middle of the Amazon Rainforest. From here you can arrange trips into the jungle and visit local tribes who have maintained their old traditions despite the emergence of a huge new city on their doorstep. The city is nothing special but the trips into the jungle are what travellers come for and they tend to be in the region of 3 or more days if you want to head into real virgin rainforest.

suggested accommodation: Hostel Manaus, Rua Lauro Cavalcante 231

And that is it! What do you do when you're in the middle of the Amazon and need to get home? Well luckily Manaus has a much improved airport now after it was developed in time for the FIFA World Cup in 2014.

From the city there are flights to many destinations across South America and also some to Miami. If you're heading to Europe it might be best to take a flight from Manaus to Belem or Fortaleza (which are served by European charter airlines like Condor) and fly to a hub like Frankfurt, Amsterdam or Milan. Although illogical you may also find it more cost-effective to take a flight south from Manaus to Sao Paulo or Rio which have a much wider selection of flights out of South America.

3.4 The Best of the Rest

Iquitos, Peru

Certainly the Brazilian Amazon has always been the most popular way to experience the world's largest rainforest but it stretches into the majority of countries in this continent. Perhaps the most mysterious of places to indulge in a bit of an Amazonian adventure is Iquitos, Peru. It's a fair old detour off our backpacking route but if you're not planning on or don't have the funds to visit Brazil, it's well worth heading out there. As well as the obvious appeal of exploring the jungle, some travellers take a little trip to the local shaman and take the powerful hallucinogenic ayahuasca. Fasting for an entire week is encouraged beforehand but the experiences are said to be mind-blowing although certainly not for the faint-hearted!

Easter Island, Chile

To call Easter Island part of South America is pushing it a bit given it is located slap bang in the middle of the Pacific Ocean but it is owned by Chile and is a completely unique and inspiring place. One of the world's most isolated civilisations has held onto almost all of its Polynesian culture and heritage.

The easiest and more or less only way to access it and fit it into your South American backpacking route is by getting a return flight from Santiago de Chile. It is likely to set you back anything from $500-1000 with LATAM (www.latam.com) who run daily 5 hour flights to/from Hanga Roa airport on the island. There are also flights to/from Tahiti which are handy for anyone from Oceania or combining travels in South America with more in Australia and New Zealand.

The Galapagos Islands

Nature lovers won't be able to get enough of Ecuador's Galapagos Islands. Giant tortoises, sea lions, iguanas and plenty of incredible bird species can all be seen from very close proximity while slightly oddly given they lie right on the equator, there are penguins. The various islands and islets form an archipelago some 1,000 km west of the South

American mainland.

Getting there is easier than getting to Easter Island but it will still set you back a fair amount of cash. Daily direct flights run from Quito and Guayaquil. In both cases it takes about two hours and arrives at Isla Baltra Airport, which is about two hours by public transport from Puerto Ayora, the main town in the Galapagos. It is also possible to fly to San Cristobal, the other major airport but on a different island. As a foreigner you can expect to pay $250-500 return, although students can often get a discount with an ISIC card. Avianca, LATAM and a national airline called TAME (www.tame.com.ec/) run services.

Antarctica

Obviously this is not part of South America but you might be surprised by just how close to the Southern tip of the continent it is and how relatively easy it is to get there. That is if you have some significant funds. Boat trips of 10-14 days are advertised online at an eye-watering $10,000 but can often be negotiated for around $3,500 in Ushuaia, Argentina and first you have to get there which is no mean feat in itself. You also have to arrive in season which runs from November to March when boats depart regularly. The sea turns to ice during the rest of the year so it's impossible to visit.

Clearly this cost could easily work out to be similar to that of the entire rest of your trip but visiting Antarctica is something very few people ever do and will certainly be something you'll remember for the rest of your life.

Venezuela & Paraguay

It may seem odd to link these two countries together that in reality are nowhere near each other. The reason being that of the main South American countries these two are by some distance the least visited.

Venezuela is considered expensive for foreigners, dangerous and unwelcoming. There is some truth to all of that but it certainly isn't the whole picture. All big cities in South America have their dangers and Caracas is certainly no different but it's not the case all over the country by any stretch of the imagination. If you can get your hands on local currency via the black market, Venezuela can actually work out to be extraordinarily cheap so more adventurous travellers looking to escape the gringo trail may want to consider it.

Highlights include Carúpano which has beaches to rival anything you'll find on the continent and with the longest Caribbean Sea coastline of any country, there are plenty more brilliant beach destinations. Inland, you can find a fair dose of adventure with the lively university town of Merida perhaps the highlight and a real hotspot for adrenaline pumping outdoor activities.

Paraguay meanwhile is more tranquil and much cheaper but is perhaps harshly considered to be the least interesting from a traveller's perspective. While it may lack an inspiring historical site like Machu Picchu or a vibrant city like Rio de Janeiro or Buenos Aires, Paraguay is not without its charms.

A highly religious country, Paraguay may not have the Inca trail, but it does have the Jesuit trail which hits its peak at the historic town of Encarnación close to the Argentine border. For the more active you can try various watersports on Lake Ypacarai near the capital Asunción.

Perhaps the biggest appeal here though is that by going anywhere in Paraguay you are treading off what is becoming an increasingly well-trodden backpacker trail and venturing into the South America that few foreigners see. Perhaps you have to look a little harder to discover its hidden gems but with over 20 different indigenous groups living in Paraguay today, many of whom speak Guarani more so than Spanish, it can be an intriguing place to spend some time if you make the effort to try and understand it.

French Guiana, Guyana and Suriname

Again French Guiana, Guyana and Suriname don't receive much in the way of backpackers although largely because they are hard to get to by land. These three countries have stronger ties to Europe than their South American neighbours which have long since gained their independence from Spain and Portugal and geographically at least it may make sense to start or end your trip here if you are from Europe and one or more of these countries appeals.

With a combined population of around 1.5 million there is little to nothing in the way of modern facilities outside of the capitals, especially in French Guiana which is very rural. Almost all the appeal of these countries is of the natural variety and there are some incredible places to visit. Kaieteur Falls in Guyana for example is a breath-taking 250 metre waterfall (5 times the size of the Niagara Falls). All three have fine Caribbean beaches and large rarely discovered jungle regions while Suriname has some fantastic nature reserves which are great places to discover rare bird and monkey species.

4) Visas & Border Crossings

4.1 Entry Requirements

The entry requirements for any country are dependent on your nationality. In this section we will indicate the entry requirements in South America for citizens of USA, Canada, Australia, UK, Germany and Ireland. The rules are generally the same for all EU citizens (Schengen area) so if you are from another country in the EU, use Germany as your guide.

In the majority of cases no visa is required and you can just rock up to the border, get your passport stamped and stay for anything from 30 to 180 days depending on the country. In cases where a visa is required you should contact an embassy or consulate of the country you want to visit.

If you're from another country to those listed, you can find out where in South America you will need a visa by using the visa check tool on our website - www.myfunkytravel.com/visa-check-tool.html

The information in this section is correct as of November 2018. Minor changes do take place from time to time so double-check before you travel to a new country.

Colombia

UK citizens - No visa required for stays of up to 90 days.

USA citizens - No visa required for stays of up to 90 days.

Canadian citizens - No visa required for stays of up to 90 days. Canadians must pay a fee of 190,000 Colombian pesos (roughly 80 CAD) on arrival.

Australian citizens - No visa required for stays of up to 90 days.

German citizens - No visa required for stays of up to 90 days.

Irish citizens - No visa required for stays of up to 90 days.

Ecuador

UK citizens - No visa required for stays of up to 90 days.

USA citizens - No visa required for stays of up to 90 days.

Canadian citizens - No visa required for stays of up to 90 days.

Australian citizens - No visa required for stays of up to 90 days.

German citizens - No visa required for stays of up to 90 days.

Irish citizens - No visa required for stays of up to 90 days.

Only citizens of 13 countries in the whole world need a visa to enter Ecuador!

Peru

UK citizens - No visa required for stays of up to 183 days.

USA citizens - No visa required for stays of up to 183 days.

Canadian citizens - No visa required for stays of up to 183 days.

Australian citizens - No visa required for stays of up to 183 days.

German citizens - No visa required for stays of up to 90 days within any 180 day period.

Irish citizens - No visa required for stays of up to 183 days.

Peru also has a relaxed policy although there is a tendency amongst border officials to only stamp 30 or 90 days. Make it clear you will be there for longer if this would be a problem and they should stamp the full amount.

Bolivia

UK citizens - No visa required for stays of up to 30 days (can be extended to 90 days, free of charge).

USA citizens - VISA REQUIRED. It can in theory be obtained on arrival for a fee of $160. However the US embassy advises you to get one before travelling which could be done at home or in a neighbouring country.

Canadian citizens - No visa required for stays of up to 30 days (can be extended to 90 days, free of charge).

Australian citizens - No visa required for stays of up to 30 days (can be extended to 90 days, free of charge).

German citizens - No visa required for stays of up to 30 days (can be extended to 90 days, free of charge).

Irish citizens - No visa required for stays of up to 30 days (can be extended to 90 days, free of charge).

Chile

UK citizens - No visa required for stays of up to 90 days.

USA citizens - No visa required for stays of up to 90 days.

Canadian citizens - No visa required for stays of up to 90 days.

Australian citizens - No visa required for stays of up to 90 days. Australians must pay a reciprocity fee of US$117 if arriving by air but there are no such charges at land borders.

German citizens - No visa required for stays of up to 90 days.

Irish citizens - No visa required for stays of up to 90 days.

Argentina

UK citizens - No visa required for stays of up to 90 days.

USA citizens - No visa required for stays of up to 90 days.

Canadian citizens - No visa required for stays of up to 90 days.

Australian citizens - No visa required for stays of up to 90 days.

German citizens - No visa required for stays of up to 90 days.

Irish citizens - No visa required for stays of up to 90 days.

Canadians and Australians no longer need to pay reciprocity fees to visit Argentina.

Uruguay

UK citizens - No visa required for stays of up to 90 days.

USA citizens - No visa required for stays of up to 90 days.

Canadian citizens - No visa required for stays of up to 90 days.

Australian citizens - No visa required for stays of up to 90 days.

German citizens - No visa required for stays of up to 90 days.

Irish citizens - No visa required for stays of up to 90 days.

Brazil

UK citizens - No visa required for stays of up to 90 days.

USA citizens - VISA REQUIRED

Canadian citizens - VISA REQUIRED

Australian citizens - VISA REQUIRED

German citizens - No visa required for stays of up to 90 days during any 180 day period.

Irish citizens - No visa required for stays of up to 90 days.

Brazil has recently introduced an e-visa system with mixed results. In theory you pay a US$40 application fee plus a small service charge, upload scans of your passport and you should be issued with a pdf copy of your visa within a week, which you should print out and take with you. This can be arranged with VFS Global (www.vfsglobal.com/Brazil-eVisa).

It's worth applying several weeks in advance in case of any problems and you can also still just go to a Brazilian embassy or consulate in person to arrange it.

Paraguay

UK citizens - No visa required for stays of up to 90 days.

USA citizens - VISA REQUIRED. Should be obtained in advance unless arriving at Silvio Pettirossi International Airport where a 90 day visa on arrival is issued for US$160.

Canadian citizens - VISA REQUIRED. Should be obtained in advance unless arriving at Silvio Pettirossi International Airport where a 90 day visa on arrival is issued for US$150.

Australian citizens - VISA REQUIRED. Should be obtained in advance unless arriving at Silvio Pettirossi International Airport where a 90 day visa on arrival is issued for US$135.

German citizens - No visa required for stays of up to 90 days.

Irish citizens - No visa required for stays of up to 90 days.

Same-day visas can usually be issued at most Paraguayan consulates. You may need to show copies of passport photos, proof of onward travel and proof of sufficient funds.

Venezuela

UK citizens - No visa required for stays of up to 90 days.

USA citizens - VISA REQUIRED. Should be applied for in person at a Venezuelan consulate. The cost is $40 and it is valid for 90 days in Venezuela within a 1 year period.

Canadian citizens - No visa required for stays of up to 90 days.

Australian citizens - No visa required for stays of up to 90 days.

German citizens - No visa required for stays of up to 90 days.

Irish citizens - No visa required for stays of up to 90 days.

French Guiana

UK citizens - No visa required for an unlimited period (will most likely change post-Brexit).

USA citizens - No visa required for stays of up to 90 days within a 180 day period.

Canadian citizens - No visa required for stays of up to 90 days within a 180 day period.

Australian citizens - No visa required for stays of up to 90 days within a 180 day period.

German citizens - No visa required for an unlimited period.

Irish citizens - No visa required for an unlimited period.

A visit to French Guiana is essentially very similar to visiting France in terms of its visa requirements with EU citizens able to stay as long as they like.

Guyana

UK citizens - No visa required for stays of up to 90 days.

USA citizens - No visa required for stays of up to 90 days.

Canadian citizens - No visa required for stays of up to 90 days.

Australian citizens - No visa required for stays of up to 90 days.

German citizens - No visa required for stays of up to 90 days.

Irish citizens - No visa required for stays of up to 90 days.

Suriname

UK citizens - VISA ON ARRIVAL*

USA citizens - VISA ON ARRIVAL*

Canadian citizens - VISA ON ARRIVAL*

Australian citizens - VISA REQUIRED. Contact your nearest Surinamese representation for more info.

German citizens - VISA ON ARRIVAL*

Irish citizens - VISA REQUIRED. Contact your nearest Surinamese representation for more info.

*A visa on arrival (tourist card) is granted at Amsterdam Schiphol Airport for €35 or at Johan Adolf Pengel International Airport in Suriname or any Surinamese representation abroad for US$40. This grants you a 90 day stay in the country.

See the following page for a list of Surinamese embassies and consulates around the world - www.embassypages.com/suriname

4.2 Border Crossings

Crossing borders in South America is usually relatively hassle-free. Besides the odd regional scuffle, this has been a remarkably peaceful continent since colonial times ended and countries generally have a good relationship with each other so there are no highly charged border crossings to deal with. Travellers of many nationalities can get around almost all of South America without ever needing a visa or having to pay an entry/exit fee (see section 4.1) so often you can get in and out of a country in no time at all.

What happens at the border?

The basic procedure is to find the emigration building of the country you are leaving, queue up a bit and get an exit stamp in your passport. Then walk 50-100 metres (sometimes more) to the immigration building of the new country and get your entry stamp which should state how many days you are allowed to stay in the country for. Occasionally both can be done within the same building while in some rare cases the border checkpoints are actually several km apart in which case you may need to get a taxi or shared minibus from one to the other.

If you're on an international bus service, the bus will stop at both checkpoints where everybody gets off and completes immigration and emigration procedures. In some cases they may make you change onto another bus at the other side of the border in which case you will need to transport your luggage over but this should be made clear by the bus driver or his assistant. If not you just leave your backpack in the hold for the duration of the trip. Make sure you have your passport and any important documents with you when you board the bus though as the driver won't be best pleased if he has to open up the hold at the border and take out all the bags just to find your passport.

Even if you don't need a visa you probably will have to fill out a brief arrivals form in the new country and you should hold onto to the departure form which you usually are issued with at this point (keep it with your passport). You will have to fill that in and show it when leaving the country and if you manage to lose it, you could in theory end up getting fined.

Important Things to Remember

It is important you ensure you have both an exit and entry stamp in your passport at every border crossing you pass through. The borders are rarely guarded by soldiers or have large fences or anything like that so it is usually possible to just walk over the border without stopping at either point but it could land you in a lot of hot water down the line if you fail to go properly through both checkpoints. Luckily the Spanish words for emigration and immigration (emigración & inmigración) are very similar to the English so it should be blatantly obvious where you need to go.

Always check before heading to a border whether or not you need a visa for the new country, as this is something you will almost certainly have to sort out in advance given few land border checkpoints issue visas on the spot. They will expect you to have it and won't stamp your passport if you don't.

Also be wary of how long you are allowed to stay in each country and make sure you don't overstay your welcome as this can lead to a heavy fine. As you can see from the previous section, 90 days is fairly typical but there can occasionally be some variation even within a country and sometimes (especially in Bolivia) you get the feeling the number of days you are granted just depends on what kind of mood the border guard is in!

One final point that you may not have considered and only really applies to people who have done a lot of travelling. That is to make sure you have many blank pages in your passport before heading to South America as once you get down to the final completely blank page, technically you can be refused entry into new countries. Likewise ensure your passport isn't going to be within six months of expiry at any point during your trip. Apply for a new passport before travelling if either will be the case.

Border Crossing Tips

There are international bus services in South America but they are usually very slightly more expensive. If you are really on a tight budget it is often best to first get a bus to the border town, then get off the bus and walk or take a taxi to the actual border crossing and then do likewise on the other side of the border. If you spot any other travellers heading the other way it might be worth stopping them and exchanging tips on taxi fares, distances to bus stations and suchlike as there are often people (especially taxi drivers) who will happily rip off newbies in their country as they use the local currency for the first time. Do your research before doing it independently also as some borders do close at night which would leave you stranded at the border if you arrive too late. The international services are certainly the most hassle free options so you will need to make a judgement call as to whether it's really worth doing it your own way.

When it comes to arrivals forms you may notice they have a tendency to ask questions that your average 'go with the flow' backpacker isn't able to answer. For example they may want the address of your first night's accommodation and the date you are leaving the country.

If you don't know where you're staying, just scribble down the name of some hostel you've heard of as they rarely actually bother to read them. You may not be asked for your departure date, but if you are then consider how long you are planning on staying and then add perhaps another couple of weeks. This is because for example if you say 10 days they may only stamp your passport for 15 days rather than the usual 30 or 90 and then you're a bit restricted when it comes to staying longer if you fancy it.

This is in truth rare and typically everyone just gets the same stamp but you've nothing to lose by exaggerating the length of your likely stay (provided it is within the time limits stated in the previous section).

Don't simply put 'I don't know' even if it's true as this may draw attention to you and they may be suspicious about your intentions.

Most border guards are not highly motivated and just want things to go as smoothly as possible so don't create extra hassle for them. Just give them what they want. In other words a piece of paper with writing in all the correct places. Most arrivals forms are in Spanish and may or may not have an English translation. If in doubt then ask someone to translate where possible or learn the basic phrases that appear on these things (Name, Date of Birth, Arrival Date, Departure Date, etc).

If you're on an international bus service don't go wandering too far from the bus at the border even if you have completed your immigration and emigration and are waiting for others. Travellers have been left stranded at border crossings before while their belongings hurtle a few hundred kilometres down a monotonous stretch of South American highway. Needless to say this isn't a cool situation to find yourself in.

Finally you will soon become aware, if you're not already, that borders do attract some sketchy characters and if anyone pressures you into doing anything you don't want then just be polite but firm and move on. 'No Gracias' may come in handy here.

It's probably not the best place to change money either but if there's no ATM nearby (there usually is) you may have no choice. In which case make sure you have a strong grasp of the exchange rates with your own currency and preferably the currency of the country you have just left. There are usually people hanging around at the border offering currency exchange and one advantage of using them to get your first stash of new money is that they will normally accept your coins from the country you just left whereas more official currency exchange places often don't accept them.

4.3 Getting to/from Central America

The cultural similarities between Central and South America mean the two are often grouped together as one region and travellers frequently visit both during the same trip.

Despite a land border existing between Colombia and Panama it is virtually impossible to go from South America to Central America by land. The thin strip that connects the two is entirely jungle and the region known as the Darien Gap has no roads. Although some foolhardy souls do cross (almost always with the help of local guides), it is a long and tiring 80 km trek and the region has traditionally been a stronghold of the Colombian FARC rebels who have been known in the past to kidnap people attempting the crossing. A treaty was signed in 2017 between FARC and the Colombian government but some FARC dissidents remain active.

Therefore unless you are a little bit bonkers the only real options are as follows:

Boat Crossing

There are many private boats and yachts that leave Cartagena in Colombia for Panama each week and if you make some enquiries in hostels around the town you can probably find one that will let you on board (for a price of course). Casa Viena in Cartagena (www.casaviena.com/cartagena-hostel.html) is a good place to go for info.

Another option is to take the scenic route and what is usually a 4 day trip including a stop in the beautiful San Blas Islands in the Caribbean. This is unlikely to be the cheapest way but it will certainly be the most memorable and one of the companies that does this trip is San Blas Adventures (www.sanblasadventures.com/boat-colombia-to-panama) although they do seem to have recently upped their prices to $399 or more at peak times. You may be able to find a better deal from other companies once in Cartagena (or Panama City if you are heading the other way).

Flights

Flying usually works out to be cheapest option. Copa Airlines (www.copaair.com) seem to have the best fares with some flights under $100 from Bogota to Panama City for example while you can also fly direct from Cartagena to Panama or vice-versa. This is a big improvement on recent times when even the very cheapest flights between South and Central America were several times that figure.

Another option is to fly from Colombia or another South American country to Fort Lauderdale or Miami in Florida. From there you can connect to all of the Central American capitals as well as Cancun.

4.4 Yellow Fever Certificates & Return Tickets

Officially many countries in South America require you to have both a certificate to prove you have had the yellow fever vaccination as well as a return ticket for them to allow you to enter their country. In reality though it is highly unlikely that you will ever have to show either, certainly at land border crossings. That said it is still wise to ensure that you won't have any problems should that situation arise.

Yellow Fever Certification

The first part is easy enough. It is highly advisable to get vaccinated against yellow fever before visiting South America, regardless of whether it is an official entry requirement or not. Be sure to get the certificate once you've had the vaccination and carry it with you at all border crossings.

The official rules regarding the need for a Yellow Fever Certificate are as follows:

Yellow Fever Certificate Required:

French Guiana

Yellow Fever Certificate Required if arriving from Risk Countries (i.e. most of South America - see section 2.2):

Bolivia, Ecuador, Guyana, Paraguay, Suriname

Yellow Fever Certificate Required if arriving from Brazil*:

Colombia, Venezuela

Yellow Fever Certificate Not Required:

Argentina, Brazil, Chile, Peru, Uruguay

Colombia and Venezuela have started asking for yellow fever certification for anyone arriving from Brazil due to the recent outbreaks there.

Return Tickets

The second issue of return tickets is a little more complicated. At any one time there are thousands of travellers dotted around South America who haven't got a flight booked back to their country. Booking a return a long way in advance is quite restrictive and if you're planning to spend 6 months or more in South America then it can actually be very difficult to even find an airline willing to offer a return ticket for a trip of that duration.

So, the question is how to get around this problem. One possibility is to purchase a fully refundable ticket which many airlines do offer if you check the terms and conditions and then claim your refund when you've crossed into the final country of your trip.

The official wording is usually 'proof of onward travel or sufficient funds'. If you are unlucky enough to be asked then note that border guards are often suckers for formal looking pieces of paper. Any official looking itinerary or a recent bank statement showing you've got a bit of cash should do the job. The whole notion of proof of onward travel is a bit ridiculous given you will probably be leaving most countries on buses where it is often impossible to buy tickets online or in advance.

In reality though and partly for this reason, it is highly unlikely you will ever be asked to show a return ticket or proof of onward travel at a South American land border crossing. Taking some of the precautions listed above might be a good idea if you are still worried about it but it's not worth seriously altering your plans to observe this rarely enforced rule.

Flying between countries, things can be a little more complicated. Check with the airline that you fly into South America with to make sure they will let you board the plane with only a one-way ticket. The airlines tend to be a little paranoid about the whole return ticket requirement thing as if a country was to refuse entry to one of its passengers they would be responsible for transporting them back home.

Even though that is highly unlikely to ever happen, they can still be a bit funny about it and some airlines don't allow people to book just one-way tickets as a result. Therefore a quick phone call to the airline before booking your ticket should clarify this. The same goes for taking international flights within South America although this is pretty rare for budget travellers as the cost of those flights almost always makes the overland border crossing much the cheaper and more appealing option.

5) Budgeting

5.1 Money

Each country in South America has its own currency apart from Ecuador which uses US Dollars and French Guiana which has the Euro. US Dollars are sometimes accepted in other parts of the continent but it's not the norm. It is though useful to take some dollars with you in case you run into problems when it comes to using ATM's which can be problematic even in more developed countries like Brazil.

In rural regions and even some reasonably large towns in somewhere like Bolivia, there may only be a couple of ATM's and sometimes none at all. They frequently break down and it can be several days before someone comes to fix them so always make sure you have some cash on you, especially when entering a new country. There are also some ATM's that don't accept international cards which can be quite frustrating.

US Dollars and notes from nearby countries can easily be changed into the local currency although rates vary considerably from place to place. Coins can rarely be exchanged nor can many international currencies so it is a good idea to get a reserve stash of US Dollars before your trip or one of the main South American currencies such as the Brazilian Real.

The national currencies are as follows:

Argentina - Argentine peso (ARS)

Bolivia - Bolivian boliviano (BOB)

Brazil - Brazilian real (BRL)

Chile - Chilean peso (CLP)

Colombia - Colombian peso (COP)

Ecuador - United States dollar (USD)

French Guiana - Euros (EUR)

Guyana - Guyanese dollar (GYD)

Paraguay - Paraguayan guaraní (PYG)

Peru - Peruvian sol (PEN)

Suriname - Surinamese dollar (SRD)

Uruguay - Uruguayan peso (UYU)

Venezuela - Venezuelan bolívar soberano (VES)

As of November 2018, these are the current exchange rates:

1 US DOLLAR is worth:

36.29 Argentine peso

6.91 Bolivian boliviano

3.78 Brazilian real

672 Chilean peso

3195 Colombian peso

0.88 Euros (French Guiana)

210 Guyanese dollar

5892 Paraguayan guaraní

3.38 Peruvian sol

7.46 Surinamese dollar

32.49 Uruguayan peso

72.69 Venezuelan bolívar soberano*

1 EURO is worth:

41.42 Argentine peso

7.88 Bolivian boliviano

4.32 Brazilian real

766 Chilean peso

3646 Colombian peso

1.14 United States dollar (Ecuador)

239 Guyanese dollar

6722 Paraguayan guaraní

3.86 Peruvian sol

8.51 Surinamese dollar

37.07 Uruguayan peso

82.90 Venezuelan bolívar soberano*

1 BRITISH POUND is worth:

46.45 Argentine peso

8.84 Bolivian boliviano

4.85 Brazilian real

860 Chilean peso

4089 Colombian peso

1.28 United States dollar (Ecuador)

1.12 Euros (French Guiana)

269 Guyanese dollar

7538 Paraguayan guaraní

4.33 Peruvian sol

9.54 Surinamese dollar

41.56 Uruguayan peso

92.95 Venezuelan bolívar soberano*

There are two official rates in Venezuela, which change wildly and regularly due to economic problems and government restrictions. The rate you get for withdrawing cash from an ATM with a foreign credit or debit card is completely and utterly different to the one you get on the black market. The bolívar soberano (VES) is a new currency which was introduced In August 2018 to deal with enormous inflation although the old Venezuelan bolívar fuerte (VEF) may still be in use in some places.

If your currency isn't featured here then research this before you go and it is a good idea to make a note of the exchange rates for all the currencies in countries you are planning to visit. Remember you won't be able use mobile internet in South America unless you want to incur huge roaming charges. If you are spending an extended time in one country, consider getting a local sim once you arrive in the first town. Getting your phone unlocked before heading to the region would be a smart move.

It's especially important to be aware of exchange rates when first entering new countries as often there are people there offering currency exchange looking to make a quick buck off naive newcomers or selling drinks/snacks at vastly inflated prices. If you've not got your head around the exchange rates you can easily get ripped off. The same goes at airports across the region, with taxi drivers often adding an extra '0' on the end of fares in countries like Chile or Colombia where fares run into the thousands. Be clear on the price before getting in or insist on a metre.

You can check current rates and the exchange rates for other currencies on www.xe.com.

5.2 Typical Backpacking Costs in South America

Budgeting for a backpacking trip is always quite a difficult task and everyone has different travel habits so information on the topic is never completely reliable.

Our guidelines below give you an idea of the daily travel costs in South America. The lower figure for each country would be a shoestring budget and is based on solo travellers staying in budget hostels (either in a dorm of single room where it is cheaper to do so) and eating in local restaurants or cooking for yourself in the hostel. It allows for a bit of drinking/partying perhaps once or twice a week but not every night and not at expensive bars and clubs. It is based on moving to a new destination on average once every two or three days. It allows for basic expenses like entry into museums or some fairly cheap activities but not for big expenses like paying for long guided trips into the jungle or extreme sports like skydiving or paragliding.

The second figure is a more comfortable backpacking budget and will give you more freedom to take flights to save time and do more in the way of activities and trips.

Possible Daily Backpacking Budget (in US Dollars)

Bolivia $15-30

Paraguay $20-30

Ecuador $25-35

Peru $25-45

Colombia $30-50

Argentina $30-50

Uruguay $40-60

Chile $45-65

Brazil $45-70

Hopefully these figures should put you in at least the right ballpark and should highlight how there are quite large variations between the cheapest and most expensive countries in South America.

There can also be quite large regional variations within individual countries. For example you may find yourself spending $65 per day in Southern Chile where the cost of entering national parks and accommodation can be very high and journeys are long and costly whereas it may only be $40 per day or less if you're just exploring one of the towns and cities further North. Prices around Machu Picchu are extortionate in comparison to the rest of Peru while in Brazil there are also large variations between the richer cities and other parts of the country.

If you move around less or focus on a small part of a country then you can often get by on less than the figures quoted as transport costs are a big factor in South America. For example average costs in Peru are often cheaper than those in Ecuador but the fact that you have to travel a long way between destinations as it is such a large country puts your costs up.

Suriname, Guyana and French Guiana are not included in the table but typically they would be considered to be at the expensive end. The reason being there is little in the way of facilities catering towards budget travellers and given they are so small most visitors go for a specific purpose (e.g. a jungle expedition) rather than to just travel around like a standard backpacker which is much more feasible in the other countries. Therefore it's hard to give an average daily figure for these countries as it completely depends on the nature of your trip.

Venezuela is another country where it is virtually impossible to put an accurate estimate for and even if we did, there's a good chance economic conditions will have changed significantly by the time you end up visiting. In short, Venezuela can be ridiculously cheap if you bring cash and exchange it on the black market. Some travellers have reported spending $10/day or less there but you will also sometimes see it listed as one of the most expensive countries in the world to visit, as the official exchange rates foreigners get at ATM's or in banks are many many times worse.

Argentina is another country that is worth a mention following a major economic crisis which has led to the devaluation of their currency. To put things in perspective, when we did the 2017/18 version of this guide, $1 was worth 15.5 Argentine Pesos. Two years on and you can get 36 pesos for a dollar! That's not good for Argentina but it does mean it is much more affordable for visitors with costs now more comparable to those in Colombia or a mid-ranking South American country than its more expensive neighbours.

Possible Backpacking Budget for Entire Trip

As you can see there is quite a wide variation in average costs between the different countries in South America with Brazil almost three times more expensive than budget-friendly Bolivia, one of the many countries which it borders. Therefore if you are on a tight budget you might be wise to focus on the Andes region and perhaps do the route from Colombia down to Bolivia but missing the more expensive nations like Chile and Brazil.

An average daily expenditure for a shoestring traveller across an extensive trip in South America including visits to lots of different countries might therefore be around $30-35 per day while those on a slightly more comfortable backpacker budget (or anyone with a shorter time-frame looking to cram a lot in) might want to allow for $45 per day.

Therefore perhaps $1000 per month would be a decent target for a savvy shoestring traveller. On this basis a whole trip may cost in the region of the following:

2 months - $2000 | €1800 | £1600

3 months - $3000 | €2700 | £2400

4 months - $4000 | €3600 | £3200

5 months - $5000 | €4500 | £4000

6 months - $6000 | €5400 | £4800

Increasing that to $1300, roughly £1000 per month, would be advisable for inexperienced travellers or anyone who wants a bit more freedom to do more expensive activities and trips without having to constantly worry about costs. On this basis, a more sensible budget would be:

2 months - $2600 | €2300 | £2000

3 months - $3900 | €3450 | £3000

4 months - $5200 | €4600 | £4000

5 months - $6500 | €5750 | £5000

6 months - $7800 | €6900 | £6000

Obviously these figures are even rougher than the initial daily figures as it depends which countries you visit but it should give you an idea of how much a backpacking trip in South America might cost.

Keep an eye on what's happening with your own currency too. A messy Brexit fall-out for example could see the Pound devalue and would make the trip much more expensive for British travellers. It's probably advisable to use US Dollars as the base for all calculations.

On top of all the figures quoted in this section, you should also factor in spending a fair bit on flights to and from South America and other pre-trip expenses like travel insurance and vaccinations. So depending on where you live and the cost of these things for you, then perhaps add another $1000+ and you'll get a rough idea of how much the trip will be in total. If you've not done much shoestring travelling before then you might want to add a little on to these figures to be on the safe side but the tips in the next chapter should help you keep costs down.

It's also worth mentioning that these figures are based on solo travel. Travelling with a partner or friend should in theory help you save money as you will be able to split costs in some situations and this should bring down the overall cost of the trip slightly.

5.3 Ten Tips for Sticking to a Shoestring Budget

It's relatively rare for backpackers to choose South America as the destination for their first big trip abroad so most people on the gringo trail have some travelling experience behind them. Evenso, the challenges of backpacking around South America are very different to those in other parts of the world and by following some of these tips you should be able to get by on a tight budget:

1. Don't be too Ambitious!

Perhaps the number one mistake backpackers in South America make is to be far too ambitious in terms of trying to fit too much into a short time. Not only will this end up with you rushing around, spending far too many hours on buses and perhaps not enjoying the trip as much as you might have, it will also be expensive.

This is not Europe, Central America or even Southeast Asia where you can often just hop between countries in no time at all. Some of the destinations on our route may appear to be in the same part of one country but can still be as much as a 12 hour night bus apart with the average bus journey for anyone backpacking around South America perhaps in the region of 4-6 hours. If you only have two or three months, you'd be much wiser to focus on one part of the continent rather than try to visit all the main countries, which would be difficult to do without taking several flights and would almost certainly push you over budget.

2. Focus on the Northern Andean region

If you only have 3 months or have a limited budget then focusing solely on Bolivia, Peru, Ecuador and to a slightly lesser-extent Colombia is a sensible ploy. Following the route from Cartagena to Salar de Uyuni (Section 3.1) for example will work out much cheaper than spending 3 months in Brazil and the south of the continent. The Northern Andes region is much more budget-friendly and in truth is arguably more interesting with more indigenous history and a culture that is further removed from that of Europe and North America.

3. Learn at least some basic Spanish

South America is not a ready-made tourist paradise and the level of English spoken is low, pretty much across the board. Spanish-speakers (Portuguese in Brazil) will have a big advantage but it's pretty easy for anyone with no background in the language to learn the numbers and basics like the different types of food and drinks. This should help almost all transactions go more smoothly and reduces the chances of you getting ripped off or scammed. It will also make it easier to spot a good deal and negotiate prices for things that are negotiable. Across the course of a trip of multiple months, those kind of savings can really add up.

4. Look out for 'Almuerzo' Lunch Deals

In typical restaurants across South America, you can usually order the 'Almuerzo' which is a very cheap set lunch. You will see it advertised all over the place and it is usually a 3 or 4 course meal which varies across the continent depending on local taste buds. It can be as cheap as US$2 which is fantastic value and it should definitely fill you up.

5. Stay in Hostels with Kitchen Facilities

The almuerzo is perhaps the one exception where eating out can be cheaper than preparing food yourself. However in general it makes sense to cook a lot of your own meals and the bigger South American supermarkets typically have a similar range of products to those in Europe or North America. Therefore it's worth finding out whether a hostel has a kitchen, certainly in destinations you plan to stay for several days. Overall it can be cost-effective to pay a couple of dollars more per night to stay in a hostel that will allow you to cook your own food and drink your own drinks on site, certainly if you're looking to do a fair amount of partying.

6. Consider Camping, Couchsurfing & Hitch-hiking in the more expensive countries

If you do go to the more expensive countries then camping and couchsurfing are good ways to save on accommodation. Even dorm beds can be over $10 per night in some parts of Chile, Uruguay and Brazil so you can make some real savings if you manage to score some free accommodation. Most cities have active couchsurfing communities (www.couchsurfing.com) that will happily host you for free although it helps if you build up a profile and a few reviews before your trip. In Southern Argentina and Chile, camping is highly advisable during the summer months when it's warm enough to be outside and when accommodation in some parts of Patagonia can soar to levels that make it virtually impossible for anyone to stick to a shoestring budget.

Hitch-hiking is a good option to save money on transport which will take up a much larger chunk of your budget in South America than it would in smaller and cheaper regions like Southeast Asia for example. Obviously there are safety concerns with this in some parts of South America. Talk to staff in your hostel and do your own research beforehand. Ridesharing apps are growing in popularity in some of the more developed nations and provide an alternative option if you are getting sick of taking a bus everywhere!

7. Keep your eyes open for flight deals

Travelling around South America has got a bit easier over the past year or two thanks to the emergence of more budget airlines. This trend looks set to continue throughout 2019 and heading into 2020 and an increase in competition should help slash prices further and see airlines offering special deals. Right now international flights are still pretty expensive on the whole but in large countries like Chile and Brazil, it's well worth looking up the cost of flying for any journey that would take say 5 or more hours by bus.

If you are a bit flexible with your dates, searching for Santiago or Rio de Janeiro 'to Anywhere' on a flight comparison site like skyscanner for example, can turn up some bargain deals that will allow you to cover large distances for less than the cost of a bus. Be sure to check out the baggage costs though as there can be large extra fees for backpacks. Consider leaving some luggage in storage in a hostel if you will be returning to the city you are currently in.

For example, if you want to visit the extreme south of Chile, leave some things in Santiago and book a return flight to Punta Arenas taking only hand luggage. At the time of writing, It's not too hard to find one-way flights (3 hours 30 minutes) on that route for around $25 whereas taking the bus would cost many times that amount and take close to two days!

8. Save on accommodation by taking night buses

Where flying isn't a realistic or affordable option, night buses are a budget traveller's best friend for longer trips. You will probably end up taking many of them during your time in South America and while they can be a drag, they serve the duel purpose of getting you from A to B while also providing you with somewhere to sleep for the night without having to fork out on a hostel. 'Cama' buses have fully reclinable seats which should increase your chances of falling asleep.

9. Take advantage of Free Stuff!

Many towns and cities in South America have free walking tours for visitors. They will normally be run by young local guides so should be informative affairs and are ideal if you only have a short time somewhere and want to see and learn about the main sites. They run on a tips basis but groups are normally large enough that you won't feel under any pressure or be expected to leave a great amount. Many hostels also offer free breakfasts and some forms of day-time or evening entertainment and activities and shoestring travellers would be wise to take full advantage of anything that is included within the cost of your accommodation.

10. Hike independently where possible

There are a few areas where heading off without a guide is not advisable, particularly in the dense Amazon but in many parts of South America, there are well marked trails and you really don't need to fork out extra cash on guides. For multi-day hikes, consider leaving a large portion of your belongings in storage at a hostel in the nearest town and head off with a lightweight tent and anything you may need for the trek. This can slash your costs in rural regions where accommodation can be more expensive and where guided treks are typically beyond the budget of most backpackers.

6) Fiesta!

6.1 Top 10 Festivals - Where & When

Tapati Rapa Nui - Easter Island, Chile

1st-16th February 2019, Exact dates TBC for 2020

Perhaps the best time to visit curious Easter Island is during early February each year when for two weeks local customs and the islanders' intriguing history is celebrated. Although the festival is for locals and it's not something you can easily participate in, visitors are welcome and the spectacle is memorable. The two week festival is a test of masculine strength and feminine poise and grace with events based on ancient sports that require extreme fitness while the girls compete in various dance competitions to be crowned queen of Tapati.

Fiesta de la Virgen de Candelaria - Puno, Peru & Copacabana, Bolivia

2nd February 2019 & 2020 (Some celebrations either side of the 2nd)

This celebration takes place in the main towns on the banks of Lake Titicaca that crosses the Peru-Bolivia border. Puno and Copacabana are only a couple of hours or so away from each other so it is easy to take in the festivities in both towns if you happen to be in this beautiful corner of South America in early February. It's a big deal in Bolivia especially and honours their patron saint, the Virgen de la Candelaria. February 2nd is the main day but it's far from just a serious religious festival and is celebrated with traditional Aymará music, dance, fortune telling and of course plenty of alcohol. On the third day in Copacabana, 100 bulls gather along the Yampupata Road and a mixture of the town's most drunk and stupid try to evade their giant horns.

Carnival - All over Brazil but best in Rio, Salvador or Olinda

1st-9th March 2019, 21st-26th February 2020

Almost certainly the most famous of all the festivals in South America and with good reason. Rio's Carnival attracts most of the international attention but it has many fitting rivals across the country. Salvador, the birthplace of Samba has a fun-fuelled week of festivities which are every bit as wild and on an even bigger scale than those in Rio. Olinda, near to Recife has a slightly different vibe with most of the events taking place during the day but the beautiful winding streets of its old town provide the ideal backdrop. It's very possible to experience more than one of these in the same trip. For example you could spend the first few days in Rio and then fly to Salvador or Recife.

Semana Santa - Ayacucho, Peru

15th-21st April 2019, 6th-12th April 2020

The week leading up to Easter is known as Semana Santa in Spanish speaking countries and it is taken very seriously in Peru and especially the town of Ayacucho. It is a fairly solemn affair with religious processions taking place all week before it all explodes into one huge fiesta on the evening of Easter Sunday. The resurrection of Christ is celebrated with dawn fireworks (of course) and it's an all-round raucous, wild party in complete contrast to the week that goes before it.

Corpus Christi - All over but big celebrations in San Francisco de Yare, Venezuela & Mahuayani, Peru

20th June 2019, 11th June 2020

This Latin ritual is a religious festival but is celebrated differently all over the continent. One of the best places to be is San Francisco de Yare in Venezuela where it is known as Diablos Danzantes. Basically the locals dress up in devil costumes and dance through the streets which makes for a weird but wonderful spectacle. This day is all about the battle between good and evil but over in Mahuayani, Peru there are no devils to be seen. Instead they don their tribal clothes and brave freezing winds to make a spiritual hike up a nearby mountain.

Boi Bumba - Parintins, Brazil

28th-30th June 2019, Exact dates TBC for 2020

If you want a unique festival experience that hardly any other travellers or foreigners make it to then look no further than the Boi Bumba Folklore festival in the heart of the Amazon. So remote is the city of Parintins on the banks of the Amazon River, it can take as much as two days to get here via riverboat from the nearest big city which is Manaus and there are no roads into town. Those who make it will be rewarded with a frenetic and boisterous Brazilian party which is based around a competition between two sides retelling a famous local folklore with elaborate parades, dances and seemingly as few clothes as possible. See www.boibumba.com.

Inti Raymi - Cusco, Peru

24th June 2019 & 2020

This is a celebration of the winter solstice in the ancient city of Cusco in Southern Peru. Its main purpose is to worship the Incan god and it includes enormous feasts, historical re-enactments and festive music. The main event is a daylong celebration of all the above but more relaxed celebrations take place in the city in the week leading up to Inti Raymi.

Tango Festival - Buenos Aires, Argentina

15th-28th August 2019, Exact dates TBC for 2020

One of the world's most provocative and sexual dances is celebrated each August in the very city where it began with the Tango Buenos Aires Festival. The festival is split into two parts with the first nine days meant for the amateurs and at times you can see or even join the tens of thousands dancing tango in the streets of BA. After that things get more serious with the Tango World Championships in Luna Park as the world's best tango dancers strut their stuff to huge crowds.

Feria de Cali - Cali, Colombia

25th - 30th December 2019 & 2020

The passionate city of Cali holds a giant celebration between Christmas and New Year. Although its origins were as a more typically Spanish affair with bull-fighting and other events more fitting to colonial era Colombia, it has developed a more local flavour that celebrates the city's origins and African influences. Nowadays it is a street carnival to rival anything on the continent with Salsa beats and dance the focal point. Colombians certainly know how to party so get ready for a wild week of festivities.

Reveillon - Rio de Janeiro, Brazil

31st December - 1st January 2019 & 2020

Want to go to the world's biggest beach party? Look no further. Upwards of 2 million people cram onto Copacabana Beach to see out the old year and welcome in the new with the mother of all parties. Fabulous food, fireworks, live music and plenty of drinks are all part of the deal as the party goes on until the sun rises above the stunning bay and revellers begin to head home or just sleep it out on the beach. One way or another it will be a New Year's Eve you will never forget.

6.2 Best Party Destinations

South America loves a good fiesta and wherever you are, you're unlikely to be far from one. However the continent doesn't boast many places with an enormous backpacker party scene which you certainly get in other parts of the world but there are one or two spots that have become hubs for party-seeking travellers.

Rio de Janeiro, Brazil

South America and perhaps the world's most famous party city is Rio de Janeiro. The setting is unrivalled with miles of long white sandy beaches, lined with everything from budget beach bars to exclusive clubs. Whether you want to party in more upscale joints in Ipanema or want the local experience of a night out in Lapa, you'll find your place here. Carnaval is the best time to visit when the whole city comes out to soak up the vibrant atmosphere but at any time of year you won't struggle to find a good time after the sun has disappeared behind Sugarloaf Mountain.

Buenos Aires, Argentina

The Argentine capital always leaves a strong impression on visitors and usually it is an extremely positive one. People know how to party here but they don't start till very late which can come as a shock to the unaccustomed. Bars and clubs are often deserted until well past midnight and the city's most popular night spots don't really get going until well into the early hours of the morning (3:00 a.m. onwards). This is a truly 24 hour party city with an enormous range of options, far greater than you would find even in Rio for example.

Montanita, Ecuador

This is perhaps as close as South America gets to the chilled out Thai Island backpacker party vibe that anyone who has travelled much in Southeast Asia will know all about. Mancora in Peru is perhaps the only fitting rival in terms of a beach-town almost taken over by travellers looking to party but Montanita is much nicer. It is only a small village but with sunny beaches, rustic accommodation, a multicultural crowd and varied and vibrant nightlife you are guaranteed to have a good time. Prices are low, the booze flows and pretty much anything goes.

Punta Del Este, Uruguay

Uruguay's principal beach resort and a major party destination for young Argentines and Brazilians looking for some sun, sea and all-night fun. Admittedly it's only really good during the South American summer and it's not at all cheap by local standards but the beaches are beautiful and the nightlife starts and ends late in what is fast becoming one of the continent's hippest party cities.

Medellin, Colombia

What sets Colombia apart from the rest of the continent is certainly its people. They are some of the friendliest and most welcoming you will ever meet and unlike other countries, are only just getting used to the fact that foreigners visit after decades of troubles. Nowhere is that more evident than Medellin, a city which was once virtually run by the infamous Pablo Escobar and his cartel. Nowadays the narcos have gone and it pumps to the sound of salsa. If you walk into a bar or club you won't be alone for long and the ease with which you can meet locals here, even with limited Spanish makes Medellin (and Colombia in general) a great place to party.

7) Best Places to Experience Local Culture

7.1 Top 5 Places for Indigenous Culture & Ancient History

South America is home to an enormous number of indigenous groups who have, with varying levels of success, managed to hold onto their own culture and customs. Here are 5 of the best places to get to know indigenous culture and ancient South American history.

Machu Picchu & the Inca Trail, Peru

It goes without saying that the ancient Incan city of Machu Picchu high up in the Andes is a hugely significant and impressive place to visit. Taking on the Inca trail that leads up to the city is an unforgettable experience and will help you better understand the history and origins of the city. However despite its ridiculously remote location, Machu Picchu is far from a hidden secret and has become one of the most popular and well known tourist destinations in South America. As a result prices and crowds have skyrocketed but it's still somewhere not to miss.

Ciudad Perdida, Colombia

This ancient site in Colombia's Sierra Nevada is six centuries older than Machu Picchu and is a sacred place for local tribes but was only widely re-discovered in the 1970's given its location is very remote in dense jungle. Although its popularity is increasing thanks to greater numbers of travellers in Colombia, if you make the challenging but beautiful jungle trek through to the lost city, you are likely to find it almost deserted which is certainly a pleasant change to what you experience at Machu Picchu.

Otavalo, Ecuador

The town of Otavalo in Northern Ecuador is somewhere where indigenous culture is still very much flourishing. The locals (known as Otavalos) are easily distinguishable with their long hair and colourful traditional clothing. They are unique amongst many indigenous groups in South America as they have flourished economically and continue to make a good trade by selling goods in the town's bustling street markets.

Lake Titicaca, Bolivia and Peru

At almost 4,000 metres above sea level, Lake Titicaca is the highest lake in the world and certainly has a mystical air to it. Backpackers frequently list this as one of their favourite destinations in South America both because of its beauty and historical significance. Its banks and islands are the ancestral land of several of the region's indigenous groups including the Quechuas, Aymaras, Uros, Pacajes and Puquinas. Highlights include the Isla del Sol (Bolivia), the supposed Incan creation site as well as Isla Taquile, which lies on the Peruvian side of the lake and has maintained its cultural traditions for thousands of years.

Cusco, Peru

Cusco was the ancient capital of the Incan Empire and is still a large and important city in 21st Century Peru. Many travellers use it as a base for beginning their trip to Machu Picchu but there is plenty to see and do in Cusco and it is a wonderful place for learning about Incan and Peruvian history. It is home to some stunning architecture and a still thriving indigenous culture as well as plenty of interesting archaeological sites in and around the city.

7.2 Top 5 Traditional Dance Destinations

Boys and girls learn to dance from a very young age in Latin America and it is an important part of life almost everywhere. You can see it best during festival times but South Americans don't need much excuse to break out into a dance and here are 5 of the best places to witness it and perhaps even learn a few moves yourself.

Salsa in Cali, Colombia

In many ways Cali is a gritty Colombian city with little in the way of interesting sights but it comes alive at night to the sound and beat of salsa and that is what the city is best known for. There are almost always salsa bars and clubs open, certainly at the weekend and often there are even people just dancing in the street. It's a good idea to take a few classes to get to grips with what can be a challenging dance before you strut your stuff with a bunch of impossibly slick-moving Colombians.

Tango in Buenos Aires, Argentina

What started in the backstreet slums of the Argentine capital has made it to ballrooms all over the world. Tango has certainly grown into a cultural phenomenon and there is nowhere better to experience it than Buenos Aires. If you're in town in August then the Tango Festival is almost unavoidable but there are plenty of opportunities to learn or just observe throughout the year and there are frequently free performances in squares dotted all over the city.

Samba & Capoeira in Salvador, Brazil

With a very large African influence, the Brazilian city of Salvador dances to its own beat. With a diverse population, wild carnival celebrations and a vibrant live music scene, this city is considered to be one of the cultural epicentres of Brazil. Capoeira is an old martial art which takes the form of a dance and originates way back in the 16th century but is still very popular with the residents of Salvador. Like Samba, which also has African roots, there are many ways to get involved and experience it in Salvador and you frequently see people out in the streets and on the beach practicing it.

Caporales in La Paz, Bolivia

This Andean dance originated in the Bolivian capital La Paz but like many of the most popular dances in South America, its inspiration came from the African slave trade. Ancient myths and legends are still very popular in Bolivia, particularly amongst its large mining community and people often dance Caporales for the Virgin of Socavón (patroness of miners). This colourful dance is regularly performed at carnival and other festivals throughout the year.

Cueca in Santiago, Chile

Cueca is a group of musical styles and dances practiced in the south of the continent and it is considered the national dance in Chile. It is a fluid dance with many different ways of performing it and is especially prominent during national holiday celebrations in Santiago, particularly on September 18th which is the country's independence day.

7.3 Top 5 Football Cities

South America has produced the two players that are widely considered to be the greatest footballers of all time (Pele and Maradona) while Argentine Leo Messi is the best player of this generation and may even have eclipsed those two by the time his career is over.

Football, Soccer, Futbol, Futebol, call it what you will, the sport is the main passion in almost all of South America and the likes of Brazil, Argentina, Chile, Colombia and Uruguay are major forces in international football. Of the Latin countries only Venezuela doesn't seem to be so bothered about it (Baseball is the national sport there but football is growing in popularity) and all over the continent you can find skilful players, exciting football, fanatical fans and fierce atmospheres.

Buenos Aires, Argentina

Football in Argentina is more like a religion than a sport and going to a match is an incredible experience. The Buenos Aires area is home to a ridiculous 26 professional football clubs and they dominate the Argentine domestic scene.

The big two are River Plate and Boca Juniors who play each other in the 'Superclasico' which is considered by many to be the biggest local derby in the world. The pair controversially clashed in the 2018 Copa Libertadores Final for the right to be crowned kings of South America and the rivalry is thriving right now. Meanwhile the nearby city of Avellaneda in Greater Buenos Aires is home to Racing and Independiente, the most successful team in the history of the Libertadores, South America's equivalent of the European Champions League.

If you arrive out of the season, which currently runs from August to

April, then you can still take an excellent tour of La Bombonera in the colourful La Boca district, home of Boca Juniors, former club of Diego Maradona.

São Paulo (& Santos), Brazil

Although when the words Brazil and football are put together, most people immediately think of glamourous Rio, it is São Paulo that is home to the country's four most successful clubs. Palmeiras, Corinthians and São Paulo FC play within the confines of the city which is also home to the excellent National Football museum (www.museudofutebol.org.br).

You have to leave the city and head to the coast to find what historically speaking is the state and the country's most successful club. Santos seems to be a production line of the world's greatest strikers. Pele scored a ridiculous 1088 goals for the club between 1956 and 1974, a total that almost certainly will never be bettered. Current darling of Brazilian football, Neymar also progressed through the club's ranks before moving to Europe.

Rio de Janeiro, Brazil

Rio's recently renovated Maracanã hosted the 2014 World Cup Final and is one of the most famous football stadiums in the world. It is the home of many of the Brazilian national side's matches as well as club sides Fluminense and Flamengo, the most widely supported team in Brazil. The other major clubs are Botafogo and Vasco de Gama and with an enormous amount of football played throughout the year in Brazil, whenever you arrive, chances are there will be a game to attend. If that fails head to Copacabana and watch some ridiculously talented beach footballers or if you're willing to make a fool out of yourself try it yourself!

Montevideo, Uruguay

For a small country of just over 3 million people, Uruguay has an unbelievably good record when it comes to the world's most popular sport. They hosted the first World Cup and have won the tournament on two occasions, a feat only bettered by three countries and the national team still to this day receives thunderous backing at the crumbling Estadio Centenario in Montevideo. The country's domestic competitions are dominated by Montevideo clubs Peñarol, who play at Estadio Centenario and rivals Nacional. Both sides also regularly take part in continental competitions.

Rosario, Argentina

Newell's Old Boys and Rosario Central are the city's two big clubs and both attract average crowds of approaching 40,000 so there is always a lively atmosphere at matches. The Rosario clubs provide the main competition to the Buenos Aires elite and play each other each season in the Rosario derby which is another ferocious affair. Rosario is also the birthplace of Lionel Messi who played for the Newell's youth team but moved to Barcelona in his early teens and the city takes great pride in its football.

8) Best Destinations for Adventure & Nature

8.1 Five Activities for Active Travellers & Adrenaline Junkies

Rafting & Hydrospeeding in San Gil, Colombia

This town in Eastern Colombia has become what travel guides like to describe as an eco-tourist hotspot and for lovers of adventure and extreme sports you might just have found your paradise. Several of the hostels and tour companies run very cheap trips into the surrounding countryside which is home to some lively rapids where amongst other things you can try your hand at rafting as well as the ridiculously fun sport of hydrospeeding which is a bit like bodyboarding but going down a speedy river.

Paragliding in Merida, Venezuela

This old university town high up in the Andes is one of the most pleasant destinations in Venezuela and its youthful population run and take part in an array of extreme sports. Mountain-biking, white-water rafting and canyoning are all popular activities here but for the biggest thrill, throw yourself into a bit of paragliding, which if you can get over the initial fear can be an amazing experience.

Skiing and Snowboarding at Valle Nevado de las tres Valles, Chile

This is South America's largest ski resort with a huge number of slopes, chairlifts and lots of the white stuff. Its location high up in the Andes but only an hour's drive from the capital Santiago makes it also one of the most accessible places to go skiing on the continent and although some of the slopes are very challenging, they also cater for complete beginners.

Surfing in Mancora, Peru

South America's Pacific Coast is home to some enormous waves which make swimming very difficult but make for ideal conditions for surfing.

Mancora is a busy little beach town full of surfers from around the world while almost all travellers heading to Ecuador from Peru (or vice-versa) stop here for a few days. There are several hostels and surf schools on the beach that offer lessons to beginners but the conditions can be quite challenging for novices. By night Mancora is a party place with a big international crowd and nightly events in the bars and hostels.

Mountain Climbing and Horse Riding at San Pedro de Atacama, Chile

The stunning landscape around San Pedro de Atacama in Northern Chile is the perfect backdrop for all kinds of adventures. With many mountains and volcanoes rising to a summit of over 5,000 metres (oxygen masks are provided!) there are plenty of challenging hikes but they are not all as difficult as they may sound and many can be completed in a day with awe-inspiring views at the top. Horse riding around the area is also very popular and enables you to reach several more remote locations that aren't possible by car or bus.

8.2 Five Natural Wonders

The Amazon

Arguably the world's greatest natural wonder, the Amazon rainforest makes up a huge chunk of this continent (around 40%) and forms part of most of the countries in it (only Argentina, Uruguay, Paraguay and Chile do not have an Amazonian region). From a traveller's perspective, its size is both a blessing and a curse. Wherever you are on the continent except the far south, you're not too far away from the Amazon so there are plenty of different ways and places to get a taste for the world's most diverse biological area. However getting deep into the Amazon is a much more challenging task and only really possible in Brazil where it can take up to a week to take the boat down the vast Amazon River into the heart of the jungle.

Patagonia, Argentina & Chile

In complete contrast to the Amazon, Patagonia is cold and rugged but equally spectacular and almost as big! This region forms much of Southern Argentina and Chile and is home to vast glaciers, beautiful lakes, stunning mountain ranges, amazing nature and very few people. If you make it all the way to the extreme south, you reach the island of Tierra del Fuego and Ushuaia, the southernmost city in the world, which is just a short ferry ride away from the world's forgotten continent, Antarctica.

Salar de Uyuni, Bolivia

Bolivia is an incredibly diverse place with plenty of natural wonders. The highlight is surely the Salar de Uyuni, the world's largest salt flats. While it may not sound particularly exciting written down, the scale of it is incredible. As you approach the middle, suddenly all you can see in all four directions is a vast whiteness. Photographers flock from all over the world to take some spectacular shots and it is an essential stop on the backpacking trail in Bolivia.

Parque Nacional Tayrona, Colombia

This delightful national park on Colombia's Caribbean shores is home to some of the most stunning coastline and best beaches in South America. By night you can sleep in hammocks and fall asleep to the warm breeze of the Caribbean Sea while days can be filled by exploring the mountains and trekking to tiny villages in the park or by simply relaxing on the beach.

Iguacu Falls (aka Iguazu Falls), Brazil, Argentina & Paraguay

Some of the world's most impressive waterfalls can be found where three countries converge in the centre of the continent. It's possible to visit Brazil, Argentina and Paraguay all on the same day and take in the stunning views from each side of what will be the most remarkable natural border crossing you will ever visit. The falls, of which there are nearly 300, cover a huge area and to put things in perspective they are served by two separate international airports and are certainly one of South America's most amazing natural wonders.

9) First Time Travellers in South America - Frequently Asked Questions

9.1 Buses & Getting Around

How do you travel from place to place?

South America barely has any form of intercity rail network and while changes are coming in the air, regional flights are still mostly expensive so if you are a budget traveller, you're going to have to get used to travelling on South American buses.

When you want to go to your next destination, find out bus times in advance at your hostel or via any other reliable source and head to the bus station, which is often quite a distance from the town centre, half an hour or more before the departure. More popular routes have regular buses all day and all night. When it comes to buying tickets find the stall of the company that runs the route and get out your best Spanish. If you speak none learn the basics for booking bus tickets as you will need it many times. It's very rare that the person at the counter will speak English.

Some pointers:

Solo ida - Only one way

Ida y Vuelta - Return

Cuanto Cuesta? - How much does it cost?

(Try to learn the numbers and times too!)

It is rarely ever necessary to book tickets prior to your trip and services are often pretty regular in the very unlikely event that one is completely sold out. You might though want to consider advanced booking during festivals and national holidays as more people travel then.

Other options besides buses include hitch-hiking which is very common in Chile and Argentina especially but may not be advisable further north. It is a nice way to meet some locals and save time as well as money. Some travellers also go for a Che Guevara-inspired motorcycle trip which would be one hell of an adventure and gives you a bit more freedom to visit more places. You could also buy a cheap car or van if you are with friends and it might not be a bad idea if you're planning a long trip around the continent.

What are the buses like? Do they have toilets? Do they stop for breaks?

They come in all shapes and sizes. The best ones are modern double decker sleeper coaches that are as good as and probably better than anything you'll find in Europe or North America. The worst ones can be pretty shabby affairs that give you the distinct impression they could break down at any moment.

Getting a bus can be a hit or miss experience bordering from pleasant efficient air-conditioned services to uncomfortable journeys on buses that hurtle around blind bends and run dangerously close to the edge of gigantic Andean cliffs (Ecuador and Peru are particularly notorious for this). You've not properly travelled in South America until you've feared for your life at least once!

Buses typically stop every few hours for a break at a service station or roadside cafe and the driver will announce how long the stop is going to be. In some countries people will board the bus selling food and drinks at various intervals which can be handy. Normally they do have toilets but you may have to ask the driver or his unnecessary and likely very bored assistant for the keys.

Also be warned that the buses that do have air conditioning will make sure you know about it! In other words they power it up so much that you may freeze to death. Therefore it's a good idea to take some warmer clothes out of your backpack before you plonk it in the luggage compartment or you may have a seriously cold 8 hours ahead of you.

Are there night buses? What are they like?

Yes there are many night buses and they are a popular way to do many of the trips in our backpacking route and others around the continent. Night buses have many advantages if you are lucky enough to be able to sleep through coach journeys. Firstly they are generally much quicker as there is hardly any traffic on the roads and they also allow you to save money on a night's accommodation.

If you're not a good sleeper and even if you are, many night buses have 'semi-cama' and 'cama' options which a little deceptively translates to semi-bed and bed. Standards and comfort levels vary from country to country and between different bus companies but basically 'semi-cama' means you can recline your seat much further back than your average one. 'Cama' enables you to fully recline it and obviously you will have more space. Prices are usually higher though if you opt for either but it might be a wise move if you want to achieve anything the next day and it often includes a drink and a sandwich if you get the midnight munchies as well as a blanket.

9.2 Local Lingo

Can you get by in South America without speaking Spanish?

It's possible to get by with little to no Spanish but it's very difficult if you go away from the most popular travel destinations (which is basically 99.9% of the continent). Most people in South America do not speak English and the few that do will attempt to communicate with you in their native tongue before reverting to English. This isn't like Europe or much of Asia where English is widely spoken and the de-facto language for most travel situations.

Therefore it is important that you learn some basic phrases and expressions before you go, especially for dealing with buying bus tickets and reading menus. You may have more joy in hostels where the staff are often foreign but many of the real budget places are local-run and don't employ English speaking staff.

To really get the most out of your time in South America then try to reach a level that at least allows you to communicate properly and have basic conversations.

What about Brazil?

Spanish and Portuguese are broadly speaking similar languages so if you speak some Spanish that will certainly help in Brazil although learning a bit of basic Portuguese would make life a lot easier. Like the rest of the continent few people speak English in Brazil but the natives here are more used to the fact that foreigners don't speak their language so tend to be a bit more understanding and patient. Portuguese is if anything a harder language to learn than Spanish but if you're planning on spending much time in Brazil, particularly outside of Rio, then learning some will again lead to a much more rewarding experience.

I don't speak any Spanish or Portuguese! How do I learn without spending a fortune on classes?

One good option is to take a week or two of intense Spanish (or Portuguese if you're going to Brazil) language classes at the start of your trip or even before you leave for South America. Cartagena, the first destination on our backpacking route is a nice place to do that. Classes are very affordable and it's a good way to meet some people if you're travelling alone in those early days which can be the most daunting.

Another excellent (and free) option is to download the Duolingo app (www.duolingo.com) on your phone. It enables you to learn new languages at your own pace via a range of skills exercises starting from the very basic phrases and working up. Some people claim they have become reasonably proficient at languages purely by using it. It also serves as a form of entertainment during quiet moments in your hostel or waiting for transport and it can become quite addictive!

Bigger cities might have language exchange or international events which are a good way to meet some locals to practice your Spanish/Portuguese with and these are often advertised on couchsurfing.com or meetup.com. Consider downloading both apps before you head to South America.

9.3 Staying Safe

I've heard South America's a bit dangerous. Is that true?

In parts yes South America is dangerous. However the same could be said for almost every continent, country and city in the world so why don't we all just lock ourselves indoors and never go anywhere.

The biggest problem, from a traveller's perspective at least, is probably the danger of theft. This is still, for the most part, a poor continent and foreigners make for an easy and attractive target. You should be careful to keep your belongings with you at all times and don't show off flashy electronics. Walking around taking photos on your iPad for example is just an invitation to thieves.

Although petty theft is a problem almost anywhere from the beaches to small Andean towns, the biggest dangers lie in the big cities. There are plenty of districts in the capitals and other larger cities which are basically considered no-go areas so keep your wits about you if you decide to go off on any random wanders, especially at night and preferably don't.

In and around the city centres, there are pickpockets and if you are unlucky you may encounter more direct thieves who are occasionally armed with knives or other weapons. Travellers are very very rarely the victims of violent crimes and if you are approached by anyone with a weapon, it's really not worth resisting so just hand over what you have. For this reason you should leave anything valuable safely stored away in a locker in your hostel, certainly at night and therefore the worst case scenario here is that you lose a bit of cash which really is not the end of the world.

As mentioned in section 2, there are odd instances where buses are ambushed in rural areas and then relieved of all their valuables. This is rare but travellers have had such problems in the past. It can usually be avoided by taking day buses in regions that are considered at risk of this. If in doubt ask the staff in your hostel to advise you on whether it is safe to take night buses.

If you go out partying, then chances are you will find most locals to be friendly and open to socialising with you, especially if you speak some of the local language. However after a few drinks if you start behaving in an aggressive or disrespectful way, then you are seriously asking for trouble. What might result in a bit of an argument or at worst fisty cuffs back home could end in something much more serious here.

More serious crimes that people associate with South America, such as kidnapping are largely a thing of the past. Colombia, which has always had a bad reputation for such things is now very safe in comparison to many of its neighbours although there are still one or two areas best avoided. Of course there are still violent groups within many of the countries often associated with the drug trade which is still rampant in parts of the continent and violent crime statistics are still high. This is largely gang-related and skewed by events in some dangerous city suburbs and slums which unless you are a little bit bonkers, you won't be going to.

Finally one mistake travellers sometimes make is that they are so caught up thinking about the perceived dangers that lie outside the four walls of their hostel that they immediately trust everyone they meet inside it and treat it like their own home. Leaving valuables lying around in a dorm is a seriously bad idea so don't do it. Get a private room or if you're in a dorm, lock everything valuable away in lockers.

Is it safe to travel solo in South America?

A large chunk of backpackers in South America are solo travellers. If you've not done much travelling outside your own country before it is perhaps a bold step to dive right into South America on your own. However if you have some experience of solo travel in Europe, Asia or other parts of the world and enjoyed it then there's no reason why you can't do likewise in South America.

You have to be wary of some of the dangers mentioned in the previous question but if you employ basic common sense, you should have a great trip. That's not to say everything will go smoothly and if you are travelling for a long period like 6 months then it's possible you will be the victim of theft at some point as it would be in your own country. While this is highly annoying at the time, it's not the end of the world provided you follow some basic suggestions.

For one always, keep a reserve stash of money and preferably a bank card stored in a locker in your hostel along with your passport and any other important documents. This way even if your entire wallet is stolen when you are out then you have a back-up. Just carry with you any money and things you will need for that day and avoid taking anything on your backpacking trip that you would be absolutely devastated to lose. You really don't need a top-of-the-range phone or iPod or a giant laptop when you are travelling.

When going from one town to the next, obviously you will need to take all your belongings with you. Be extra vigilant at this point and keep your valuables preferably locked away in a safe compartment of your backpack. Do your research beforehand on your next destination and if you arrive at night consider taking a taxi from the bus terminal to a hostel.

These precautions may seem a little over the top and you may be lucky and have no problems at all during your trip but it's better to be safe than sorry. Travellers in groups should also consider following them but if you are the victim of a theft and you are with a friend it is not such a problem as you can hopefully rely on them if you have money stolen or suchlike.

Is solo female travel safe in South America?

Girls frequently travel in South America alone and although from time to time you may receive some unwanted male attention, it is nowhere near as creepy as in India for example where highly inappropriate groping is not uncommon.

The main time to be careful is at night in big cities. Ideally you will make some friends in the hostel but if you do head out alone, use licensed taxis to get around and speak to the staff in your hostel for advice on where to go and where to avoid. If you go out to a bar alone (and the same goes for guys), just be sensible, keep an eye on your drink at all times and of course try not to get completely wasted. In other words do everything you should do in the same situation at home!

Also and this is very important, make sure you have the address of your hostel written down somewhere so you can get back home safely at the end of the night. Many taxi drivers won't know how to get there just on the name alone. Needless to say roaming around the streets drunk at 3:00 a.m. in the morning on your own in a South American city is not a good idea.

Another smart idea might be to find a hostel on a busy road, rather than a quieter backstreet which may look perfectly fine in the day but once night falls, begins to feel a little shady. Do your research when finding hostels and choose ones that have received positive reviews and high location ratings. Many hostels have female-only dorms which typically will be full of girls travelling alone or in small groups so you should be able to find some travel buddies that way.

Finally, If you've not travelled solo before you may not be aware that some guys that frequent hostels have shall we say, questionable intentions when it comes to befriending solo female travellers. The positive here is that it is usually easier for solo girls to make friends than solo travelling boys. The negative, you may get yourself a hostel stalker. Fun Times.

9.4 Finding Accommodation & Making Friends

How do I find accommodation? Do I need to book in advance?

Accommodation generally doesn't need to be booked in advance in South America but in any reasonably sized town it helps a lot to have an idea of where you are going to stay before you arrive. Often most hostels are located in the same area, so you can walk around and see what appeals if you don't like the look of the one you were intending to stay in.

The backpacking routes in this guide include a suggestion based on somewhere that is relatively cheap but also has received positive reviews. You can also use hostel booking sites like hostelworld.com or hostelbookers.com to find accommodation or at least see what sort of choice is out there. You don't necessarily have to book just in case your plans change.

Booking in advance and sometimes well in advance is only really advisable during big festivals or national holidays. Carnival in Brazil is a good example of this and even booking months in advance you can expect to pay several times the going rate. Weekends in the bigger cities like Buenos Aires often sees the better places sell out quickly but there is usually still an enormous range of options.

Purchasing a budget travel guidebook like Lonely Planet's Shoestring Guide will also give you a range of cheap options for most destinations but often hostels do open up and shut down at short notice so don't take everything in there as gospel. Often the cheapest places are those with no online presence whatsoever so if you speak reasonable Spanish, you can probably just ask a few locals on arrival for suggestions. These local joints aren't the best places to meet other travellers though but you can often get very cheap rooms.

Other options include camping which is very possible in more rural areas and will help you save a lot of money in countries like Chile and Argentina. You can also give couchsurfing a go which can be a brilliant way to really experience the country and its people. Finding an Airbnb (Airbnb.com) is a nice option at times too as staying in hostels for months on end can start to get a bit tedious after a while.

How do you meet locals and other travellers?

Most travel buddies are made by staying in hostels and usually in dorms although common areas or bars are also excellent places to make a friend for a few days. This can be a big concern for first time solo travellers but it's often surprisingly easy to meet other travellers as many are in exactly the same position as you.

You can also take up short Spanish or Portuguese language courses in a few places which will help you learn the lingo and hopefully give you some ready-made friends. Couchsurfing is another good way to meet locals and travellers alike. If you don't fancy staying with strangers, there are many people who are happy just to meet up and perhaps even give you a tour of their town.

These days, there are plenty of apps out there which help you meet up and/or hook up with other people near you. Some travellers in recent years have used tinder to quickly meet up with people when they arrive alone in a new city. Although it is a dating app, there is no reason why you can't use it for purely making friends but be sure to specify this in your profile and repeat it when you start chatting to someone if this is your only intention.

9.5 Weather & When to go

What's the weather like?

Weather-wise obviously there are huge variations given it is such a big continent. Very generally speaking equatorial countries like Colombia, Ecuador and Venezuela aren't subject to such major seasonal variations but further south you should certainly consider the weather when planning your trip.

If you're an outdoors person or beach lover then you'd probably want to think about avoiding Southern Chile, Argentina, Uruguay and perhaps even Southern parts of Brazil during the colder months (May to September). Certainly it gets freezing cold as you head down into the far south at this time and although prices are generally lower as you're out of season, it's not a pleasant experience. Night temperatures have been known to be as low as -20°C in Ushuaia at this time for example and are usually sub-zero with the days not much warmer.

Mountain regions are typically fairly warm and usually sunny during the day with high UV levels due to the altitude but temperatures fall rapidly as night sets in and it can also get very cold. Average temperatures in La Paz for example are consistently around 18°C during the day throughout the year but fall to just above freezing at night so you will need warm clothes if you are going to be spending much time in the Andes.

Then there is the rainy season which affects some parts of the continent but at different times. It might be very hard to avoid this altogether if you are doing a long trip in South America and it's often not that severe in any case. Amazonian areas typically experience their rainy season during the first six months of the year while areas close to the equator typically have two separate small rainy seasons a year.

When is the best time to go?

Perhaps the best advice is to decide on two or three things that are going to be the highlights of your trip and plan around that.

The Inca trail to Machu Picchu for example is said to be best in May or June, which is just after the rains have passed. Temperatures can get very cold at night (perhaps even sub-zero) as you're up in the mountains but days are typically dry and sunny although not too hot.

If Patagonia and perhaps even Antarctica is on your agenda then you should certainly think about heading there in or around the summer months (November to March). Trips to Antarctica aren't possible at other times of the year. The far south of the continent is beautiful during the winter but often bitterly cold.

The Amazon meanwhile has its dry season from July to December which despite the intense heat and humidity is considered the best time to visit for hiking as there is relatively little precipitation. The wet season (January to June) is less good for walking as you will be getting drenched on a regular basis and the forests get flooded. However higher water levels do enable boats to travel faster and deeper into the jungle so this is a better time to visit if you want to experience the Amazon but not by spending all day walking around it.

Other factors in deciding when to visit might include trying to fit in one of the major festivals and celebrations. Popular options include starting or ending your trip in Rio de Janeiro for Carnival (February or March) but you should be aware that prices of flights and accommodation will skyrocket at this time.

November to March is also a good time to hit the beach in Brazil and Uruguay. Beaches along the Caribbean coastline of Venezuela and Colombia are warm throughout the year with very little change in temperatures and although there are rainy seasons, most days are hot and sunny with the odd interruption for a short sharp shower.

10) About

10.1 About Funky Guides

Funky Guides is an offshoot of MyFunkyTravel (www.myfunkytravel.com) which offers backpacking tips, advice and articles for regions across the world.

The aim of Funky Guides is to provide cheap guides for budget travellers written by budget travellers who have had real travel experiences as opposed to professional writers. In each one you will find honest advice and suggestions and some practical information that will help both planning your trip and the trip itself go smoothly. We aim to cut down on the information-overload and summarise the most important bits.

They won't tell you where to eat, where to drink, what time to get up, what to think, where to blow your nose or anything like that. It's a mixture of basic but important information that you can easily refer to every now and then, combined with some ideas that may provide you with a little bit of inspiration that will help your trip take shape.

You can find us on facebook and twitter - @myfunkytravel

10.2 About this Guide

This guide is a new version of our previous South America Backpackers Guide. It was fully updated in November 2018 for 2019-2020. This update included a full review of every chapter with factual information such as dates and exchange rates altered. The section on shoestring travel tips is new and the result of some feedback on the previous edition. We also made several other some small changes to make the guide more up-to-date and relevant for anyone travelling in the coming year or two.

For example many of the hostel suggestions have been changed from the 2017-18 edition to take account of more recent reviews. The problem with budget accommodation, both in South America and other regions, is that places can be good one year and then rapidly go downhill if a change of ownership happens or if complacency sets in once they've got a recommendation from one of the bigger guidebooks. We'd love to hear your feedback (good/bad) if you stay at any of the places we have suggested as we aim to update this guide as regularly as possible and clearly don't want to recommend anywhere lousy.

For the record, the hostels mentioned in Section 3 have not paid anything to be featured here. They merely provide budget accommodation and have received very positive recent feedback from travellers. Likewise other travel companies and websites that are featured, are only there because they provide a useful practical service for backpackers in South America or people planning to visit.

If you still have questions about backpacking in South America after reading this guide or to get in touch with the author, you can write to - info@myfunkytravel.com. We will try to get back to you as soon as possible although this may take a few weeks at busy times.

If you found the guide helpful we would really appreciate it if you left a review on Amazon! We hope to produce more guides in the future and update this one as regularly as possible but your support is vital.

Thanks for reading and enjoy your trip! :)

Image Credits

The cover image used is of Valparaiso, Chile under the CC BY 2.0 licence:

https://www.flickr.com/photos/deensel/28299696589

https://creativecommons.org/licenses/by/2.0/

The map of South America on page 1 is via Wikicommons under the CC BY-SA 2.0 licence:

wikitravel.org/en/File:Map_of_South_America.png

creativecommons.org/licenses/by-sa/2.0

© 2018 Funky Guides

All rights reserved.
No portion of this book may be reproduced in any form without permission from the author.

Printed in Great Britain
by Amazon